Ulrich Bieber is director of a specialist tour operator. For years now, the 38-year-old graduate in Travel Economics has been visiting exotic countries regularly to discover romantic spots for wonderful honeymoons and to pave the way for valid marriages abroad. His travel tips are published in bridal fashion magazines and women's journals.
Bieber spent his own honeymoon on Mauritius. His family has grown to four in the meantime and, as he puts it, "is better catered for in a family-hotel".

Just you and me

COMPANIONS

The most beautiful places for an unforgettable honeymoon

Contents

Pacific Ocean

Caribbean

www.world-wide-weddings.com

www.uniquesailing.com

www.uniquediving.com / www.Indian-Ocean-Islands.com

Infinity Specialist Tours Ltd.
71a Bell Street, Henley-on-Thames
Oxon. RG9 2BD, England
Telephone: (01491) 571 545
Telefax: (01491) 636 159
e-mail: info@infinitytours.co.uk

Dear reader,

Are you planning your wedding and looking for ideas where to spend your honeymoon? Have you been married for a few years now but haven't gone on your honeymoon yet? Or, are you dreaming of a very special wedding abroad? Then it is well worthwhile to leaf through this book. Infinity, one of the leading honeymoon travel organisers, introduces you to some of the world's most beautiful destinations. Infinity presents wedding and honeymoon destinations – places which satisfy every taste – whether secluded islands, wild jungle-landscapes or exciting cities. And, the hotels featured are as just as interesting as the countries. Bridal couples are not only specially catered for, but frequently get to enjoy special and exclusive privileges into the bargain.

Those of you dreaming of a honeymoon and getting married in paradise will find suggestions on the following pages for special wedding-packages that make a wedding under palms or in other exotic settings possible. And, couples need not worry about a single detail. The complete organisation of the wedding rests in the hands of experienced operators.

No matter where you go and where you will exchange rings, it is worthwhile to view the www.world-wide-weddings.com website! This is the Internet address of Infinity Specialist Tours, the specialist weddings and honeymoons tour operator. The agency helps couples to plan and organise their trips and to prepare for all necessary marriage formalities. Infinity will see to it that a most wonderful day in your life and your honeymoon are unforgettable experiences.

Infinity wishes you lots of fun making your plans and realising your dreams.

Have a wonderful trip!

EUROPE

Germany

Germany, Land of Poets and Thinkers, is gaining growing esteem as a rewarding destination for tourists. This comes as no surprise because, apart from areas with charming landscapes and a moderate climate, there are many places on the World Heritage list.

Mecklenburg-Western Pomerania

Lakes, forests and lots of water: Mecklenburg-Western Pomerania is the thinnest-populated federal state in Germany and its multi-faceted natural environment presents many highly-varied opportunities for recreation and recuperation. In the north, the state is characterised by its long Baltic Sea coastline with dreamlike beaches, islands, peninsulas and steep coastal sectors such as the well-known chalk-hills on Ruegen. The Mecklenburg Lakes, a genuine paradise not only for active aquatic sportsmen, are its interior's main attraction.

The remaining landscape is marked by gentle hills, expansive fields and forests. The climate is mild; the sunniest days in Germany are counted in this region.

The historical cities, established along the trade route dating back to the 12th century, appeal to visitors with an interest in culture. Examples of these cities are the state capital Schwerin, the Hanseatic cities of Rostock, Wismar, Stralsund, Greifswald and others which offer a wide range of scenic attractions.

Schlosshotel Burg Schlitz*****

Stately residence in a beautiful environment
Hohen Demzin

The Schlosshotel Burg Schlitz now shines with a new splendour after renovation and redesign. The stately residence provides relaxation in a private atmosphere.

Accommodation & Amenities
The 14 guest-rooms and six suites are generously laid out and equipped with custom-built Biedermeier-style furniture and works of art. Exquisite Mediterranean cuisine with an Indonesian flair is served in the restaurant's Gothic-style Hall of Knights. In addition, guests are spoilt either in the Schlosscafe, on the terraces, or in the bar.

Activities
One highlight is virtually on the doorstep: The breathtaking, huge Schlosspark with its centuries-old trees, its lakes and extensive paths, which are lined by monuments, grottoes and columns, is perfect for splendid strolls or bicycle-tours. You can indulge in many forms of recreation, such as golf, archery, horse-riding, fishing and hiking in the neighbourhood. From autumn 2002, you can treat yourself to a wide range of treatments in the spa.

Honeymoon extras/weddings
Registry-office weddings take place in the idyllic small town of Teterow, six kilometres away. A limousine brings you back to the hotel.

Services included
▸ A large breakfast in the castle
▸ Marriage according to church rites in the castle's Karolinen chapel
▸ Champagne-reception following the ceremony
▸ A wedding-cake from the castle's bakery
▸ Elegant celebration in the Hall of Knights, including a five-course menu
▸ A tour of the park in a horse and carriage
Price per couple from £ 995

Prices/addresses
Overnight stay with breakfast from £ 135 per double-room.
Schlosshotel Burg Schlitz
D-17166 Hohen Demzin
Tel: +49-3996-127 00
Fax: +49-3996-12 70 70

Austria

Austria, the land of mountains, attracts numerous guests from all over the world each year who appreciate the magnificent landscape, rich culture, fine cuisine, hospitality and security. However, its diversity is reflected not only in the unique landscape but also in the heartiness of its people. Austria's central location in Europe brings together a variety of cultural streams. This creates an atmosphere of its own. Experience Austria with all of your senses: the air, the mountains, the beauty of the landscapes, the feeling of fresh lake-water on your skin!

Salisburg

Salisburg (Salzburg) is one of Austria's most popular destinations. The city is characterised by art, music and buildings that are steeped in history. Many visitors are delighted just by the first sight of the city which is surrounded by rivers and mountains. And then of course it is Wolfgang Amadeus Mozart's birthplace. The Old City sometimes looks Italian because the most important buildings were created by Italian architects in the Baroque

era. Salisburg owes its architectural style mainly to its outstanding status as the Prince Archbishop's city of residence. The bell-tower and the huge cathedral bear witness to its mighty past. What city would be more suited for a romantic dream-wedding!

Mirabell Castle

The influential Prince Archbishop Wolf Dietrich von Raitenau, who put his mark on the city like no other, had Mirabell Castle built for his mistress Salome Alt. A wedding-hall, considered one of the most beautiful in the world, awaits nuptial couples here. The castle's famous Marble Hall is the Prince Archbishop's former banqueting hall in which Leopold Mozart and his children Wolfgang and Nannerl held concerts.

Bridal couples feel in seventh heaven there, especially because the red-letter day can be arranged according to their special wishes. This ranges from all forms of musical accompaniment and numerous transportation possibilities to the suitable setting for the wedding-dinner. After the ceremony, the wedding-party adjourns to the garden amidst groups of sculptures, floral arrangements and fountains. You have a beautiful view of Hohensalzburg Fortress from there.

The bride's abduction and morning-gift

Weddings in Austria are a pretty lively affair, the bride is "kidnapped" by her friends and taken to a café or bar. The bridegroom, accompanied by the witnesses, then has to search for her in the neighbourhood pubs and bars is able to have her released only by paying the bill. On the other hand, the morning-gift, a present that the couple exchange with each other on the morning of the wedding is a sign of reconciliation. According to the legend, if the bridegroom places his under his wife's pillow, he will be blessed with a long happy marriage.

Wedding package Mirabell Castle

▶ Two nights in a luxury-class hotel in the city-centre including a sumptuous buffet breakfast
▶ A bridal bouquet of fresh flowers
▶ Limousine transfer from the hotel to Mirabell Castle
▶ Registry wedding in Mirabell Castle, musical accompaniment, floral decorations
▶ Tour in the wedding-coach through Salisburg's Old City to the hotel or restaurant
▶ Festive wedding-menu in a gourmet restaurant including cocktails and table-decoration
▶ Assistance with the registration and certification of the marriage (all local fees)

Additional services

▶ Photography service
▶ Video service
▶ Rental of a bridal gown or wedding-suit
▶ Wedding-meal for the guests
▶ Hairdo and beauty-treatment for the bride
▶ A bottle of champagne and wedding-cake in the hotel
▶ Fanfare ensemble
▶ Limousine transfer to the airport or railway-station
▶ A vintage car at extra charge instead of a Mercedes limousine

What documents are required?

▶ Passport copies and newly-issued birth certificates stating the place of birth and certified by apostille
▶ Document showing permanent address (e.g. photocopies of driver licences)
▶ Certificate of No Impediment to Marriage, certified by apostille
▶ Certificate of spouse's death if widowed (certified by apostille), or certificate of the former marriage as well as the short form of the final divorce certificate, certified by apostille, if divorced

What deadlines are to be observed?

▶ The documents must reach Infinity Specialist Tours Ltd. eight weeks before the wedding at the latest

Price per couple from about £ 1,660

The Alpine pasture Wedding

A rustic experience in an impressive setting
Salzkammergut near St. Gilgen

An Alpine hut instead of the registry, cowbells as wedding-bells. You make your vows in the idyllic surroundings of a rustic Alpine hut, nestled in lush green meadows with a wonderful view of the Wolfgangsee and the Schafberg hill.

In good weather, the marriage ceremony that is followed by a festive meal with traditional Austrian delicacies takes place in the beautifully-situated Laerchenhuette in the Salzkammergut near St. Gilgen. The lodge contains a cosy room with a wood-burning stove, rustic tables and wooden benches, which can seat up to 35 wedding guests.

However, whether you are travelling alone or only with your witnesses you are heartily welcome in the Laerchenhuette. The lodge, located at an altitude of 1,050 metres, can be reserved from mid-May to October.

Hotel Schloss Mönchstein*****

A dreamlike castle in a romantic city
Salisburg

Mönchstein Castle is a romantic, dreamlike estate with ivy-covered walls, towers and oriels. It is suitable for wedding festivities at any time of the year. In summer, you celebrate in the breathtakingly-beautiful ten-hectare Schlosspark. Umbrellas, tables and chairs are set up there so that the couple and its guests are able to enjoy the summer-wedding party in a comfortable, relaxed atmosphere. The castle atmossphere is just as romantic in winter. It is a white, warm, inviting place, especially in the snow. The elegant banqueting halls are furnished with long tables and provide room for a large number of guests in festive surroundings.

Accommodation & Amenities
Individually-styled rooms and suites await the bridal couple. The rooms are furnished with antiques from various periods, which, in combination with modern comfort, create a unique atmosphere. There is a choice between normal suites, the Royal Suite and the Prince's Suite.

Superior-, Standard- and small double rooms are also available.

Gourmets also get their money's worth in the castle's two restaurants: A highly creative Austrian- and international cuisine is served in the Paris Lodron. In the grand Maria Theresa restaurant, guests feast on the most delicious creations from the kitchen and drink selected wines amidst precious paintings, antique carpets and Renaissance furniture. Each visit is a celebration for all of the senses.

Activities

One of Salisburg's many attractions stands before the hotel-doorstep – the castle's own Schlosspark. This was generously extended in the 19th century and decorated with valuable sculptures. Katharina, wife of Tsar Alexander II of Russia, Empress Elisabeth and Alexander von Humboldt, all once guests in the castle, have strolled along its picturesque pathways.

Naturally, Salisburg also features numerous sightseeing attractions. For example, you should not miss a visit to Mozartplatz (Mozart Square) and listen to the renowned Salzburg chimes. A stroll through the Getreidegasse, with its well-preserved 17th and 18th century facades and the elaborately-decorated house- and business-signs, is also a must.

One of the most beautiful destinations for outings in the area is Hellbrunn Castle. It is one of the best-preserved testimonies to manneristic architecture north of the Alps. The water tricks and games in the Baroque garden complex that dominate the park together with grottoes and sculptures, are still just as delightful as they were in the past.

Honeymoon extras/weddings

A small bottle of champagne is placed in the room on arrival and bridal couples are automatically upgraded, subject to availability.

Prices/addresses

A night in Schloss Mönchstein costs from £ 165 per person in a standard room. A suite can be rented from £ 235.

Hotel Schloss Mönchstein
Moenchsberg Park 26
A-5020 Salzburg
Tel: +43-662-84 85 55-0
Fax: +43-662-84 85 59
www.monchstein.at

Scotland

The manor-hotel Cameron House stands directly on Loch Lomond, nestled among gentle hills, lush fields and dense forests. The ancient walls radiate history and tradition, luxury and elegance, much warmth and comfort. A tastefully-integrated pool- and fitness landscape provides relaxation and recuperation; the fascinating natural surroundings at the doorstep seem created for activities such as hiking, golf, horseback-riding or fishing.

Couples who want to tie the knot in Scotland are accommodated luxuriously in the castle, in keeping with the event. The hotel staff take very special care of them so that they are able to get ready the big day.
The most beautiful room for the fairytale wedding is the manor's library which many celebrities from all over the world have leafed through. The minister, who Scottish law permits to conduct the ceremony instead of a registrar, is happy to join international couples in matrimony. The musical setting by a bagpiper is a highlight that puts everyone involved in the right mood for the significant event.

What deadlines are to be met?
Travel reservations should be made about six weeks before starting the journey in order to be able to complete the necessary formalities smoothly.

What documents are necessary?
▶ Passport copies and birth certificates
▶ Marriage Notice Form
   (the registration form will be organised by the tour operator when the reservation is made.)
▶ If you were previously married, a certificate of divorce
▶ The death certificate of your former spouse if you are a widow or widower

Wedding package "Historical Scotland"
▶ Private transfer airport-hotel-airport
▶ Two nights in Cameron House Hotel (incl. breakfast)
▶ Bridal bouquet of fresh flowers
▶ Wedding ceremony in the hotel-library with musical setting by a bagpiper
▶ Sparkling wine and wedding-cake after the ceremony
▶ Romantic candlelight dinner in the gourmet restaurant Georgian Room
▶ incl. cover, six-course menu and festive table-decoration
▶ Champagne breakfast on the morning after the wedding
▶ Assistance with registration and certification of the marriage
▶ All local fees
Price per couple: From about £ 1,280

Italy

Italy is still the classical honeymoon land for many people. The short journey by car, rail or air from Germany, Austria or Switzerland makes it interesting for couples wishing to begin a future together in Mediterranean surroundings but not without their relatives and friends.
Veneto, the province in the rectangle between the Dolomites, the Po Valley, Lake Garda and the Adria, attracts visitors with an affinity for beautiful countryside, magnificent ancient villas, exquisite wines and exceptional cultural delights. Here you find Venice, the city of love described in numerous novels and painted by the most prominent artists of all eras.

A gift for the guests
If you are invited to a wedding in Italy, then look for a suitable present without delay. The custom is to deliver a gift long before the wedding to the family of the bride or groom, depending on with whom you have the closer relationship.
The donor is entertained there with champagne, nibbles and sweets. He or she will also be given presents in return – the so-called bomboniera. These are little, often self-made souvenirs such as small bags, tiny dolls or picture-frames. A bag of "confetti" – sugar-coated almonds – is always included.
On their wedding-day, bride and groom first see each other in the church. They already have drunk a toast to the big day with their families at home. The wedding feast begins after the ceremony and lasts into the late afternoon. The end of the feast also marks the end of the celebration.

Tuscany is equally characterized by its famous cities and the fairytale landscape of the Chianti district.
Florence, the cradle of European culture, is the provincial capital and its heartbeat.

You reach Siena province by travelling through the famous wine-growing areas of Chianti. The district extends to the border via the hilly landscape and Crete. Siena city itself is marked by its Gothic architecture. The famous Piazza del Campo, one of Italy's most beautiful squares, located in the city centre, is a sight not to be missed. Or as the italians say: "Da non perdere". The same can be said of the cathedral with its breathtaking ceiling.

Londra Palace Hotel****

Privacy in the palace
Venice

The view from all 100 windows of this small palace wanders unhindered over Venice's famous lagoon and the island of San Giorgio. The perfect viewpoint from which to absorb the beauty and romantic atmosphere of this "City of Love". No wonder that the composer Tchaikovsky was inspired to write his famous Fourth Symphony when staying in this hotel during a visit to Italy in 1877. The Londra Palace Hotel is small but a good address for

people who appreciate a personal note. It was renovated in autumn 1999 for eight million U.S. dollars by Rocco Magnolis, the architect who left his marc on Gianni Versace's boutiques, among other buildings. Magnolis set new accents with glass elements and lighting effects without breaching the neoclassical style.

Accommodation & Amenities

The hotel contains "only" 53 rooms, including 17 suites. All of them are equipped with bath, air-conditioning, telephone, mini-bar, satellite TV, radio, soundproof windows and a king-size bed. Some have a view of the lagoon.
The original 19th-century furniture and works of art give the interior a warm glow. The marble-tiled bathrooms have hairdryers, bathrobes, illuminated mirrors, heated towel-racks and a Jacuzzi-bathtub available. Room-service fulfils guests' wishes around the clock.

A dinner in the hotel's restaurant, Do Leoni, is also something special – whether in the inviting inner rooms or on the romantic terrace with a magnificent view.
The menu is rather limited but it makes the heart of every gourmet leap. The restaurant serves only choice Venetian and international specialities, accompanied by carefully-selected wines.

Activities

Because of the hotel's central location near St. Mark's Square, all important places of interest are just a short walk away. It takes only five minutes along the Riva degli Schiavoni promenade to St. Mark's Square and the city-centre. Both tourists and locals can choose from numerous typically Venetian restaurants and bars nearby for a meal or a glass of wine on mild summer evenings.
You should not fail to glance into the picturesque sidelanes off the beaten tourist track. However, Venice does not attract visitors with the arts and paintings alone; the

Venetian festivals are major events in the otherwise dreamy city. The most famous is the Carnival of Venice which attracts thousands of visitors every year. The numerous historical celebrations, when the Canale Grande just teems with boats and colourful gondolas, express pure joy for living.

The regatta on the Feast of the Epiphany, the "Marriage with the Sea" on Ascension Day and the historical regatta on the first Sunday in September are but a few. Music-lovers, friends of the theatre and film-makers all meet at the Biennale that the city hosts every two years.

Prices/addresses

Accommodation in a double-room with a view of the lagoon and breakfast costs in Londra Palace Hotel from about £ 180 per person and night.

Londra Palace Venezia
Riva degli Schiavoni
I-30122 Venezia
Tel: +39-41-520 05 33
Fax: +39-41-522 50 32

Park Hotel Siena****

Rooms with a view
Siena

The Villa Gori has been sitting atop Marciano hill overlooking Siena for almost 500 years. Today, people are still able to recuperate best from everyday stress and the big-city noise here, where the banker's family of the same name once spent the summer months in fresh rural air. The stately residence was changed into a hotel in 1960 but the architectural structure was left untouched. Now the hotel is part of the Charming Hotels chain.

Accommodation & Amenities
Situated just two kilometres from Siena, the hotel has 70 rooms and suites, all furnished modern style. The view from the windows and terraces opens onto the silhouette of the city and the hilly landscape of Tuscany. The premises are surrounded by a small forest and an English-style park.

The hotel-restaurant pampers its guests with specialities from Tuscany's cuisine. The ingredients come fresh from the vegetable-garden adjoining the hotel, its own vineyard or the nearby olive grove.

Activities
The hotel has an excellent variety of sports available. It owns a nine-hole golf course, a swimming-pool and tennis courts as well. Many sightseeing opportunities are close at hand. They include the city of Siena, which is rich in historical art-treasures, and the nearby Chianti Hills.

Prices/addresses
A night in a Standard double-room costs from about £ 99 in a Junior Suite £ 170 (both per person, with breakfast).
Park Hotel Siena
Via Marciano 18
I-53100 Siena
Tel:+39-577-448-03
Fax:+39-577-490-20

Wedding arrangement
"Picturesque Siena/Tuscany"

Siena offers a special setting for a wedding, with its Town Hall, the Palazzo Pubblico, in the centre of the mediaeval-Gothic Old City.

The wedding-hall is located on the first floor and from the window you look out onto the Piazza del Campo square where a you may toast with sparkling-wine after the ceremony. An unforgettable setting, ideal for a wedding.

What documents are necessary?
▶ Passport copies and newly issued birth certificates mentioning also place of birth
▶ Superintendent Registrar's Certificate of No Impediment to Marriage
▶ Certificate of spouse's death if widowed (certified by apostille)
▶ Certificate of the former marriage as well as the short form of final divorce certificate, if divorced

Services included:
▶ Three nights with breakfast in Park Hotel Siena
▶ Transfer from the hotel to the register-office
▶ Civil wedding-ceremony in the Sala del Concistoro in the 13th century Palazzo Pubblico including floral arrangement
▶ An interpreter during the ceremony
▶ Prosecco on the Piazza del Campo
▶ Transfer to the restaurant Al Marsili
▶ Tuscanese wedding-menu and festive table-decoration
▶ A bridal bouquet of fresh flowers
▶ Assistance with the registration and certification of the marriage
▶ All local fees

Price per couple about £ 2,240

Additional services
▶ A photographer, including 36 pictures 13x18 cm in an album, about £ 400
▶ A different hotel category is possible on inquiry

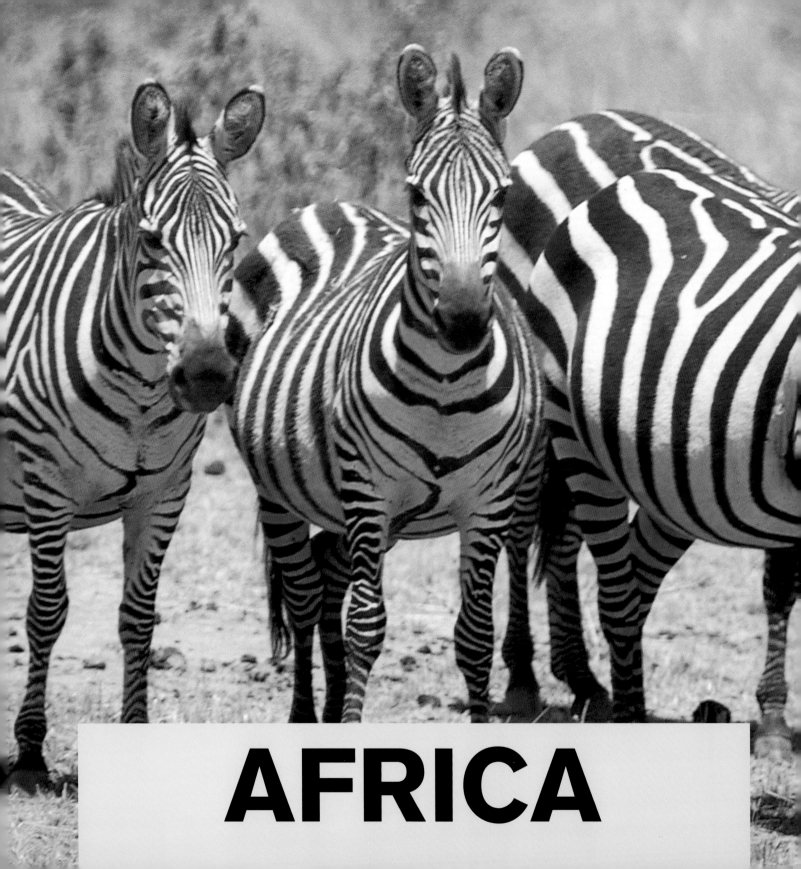

AFRICA

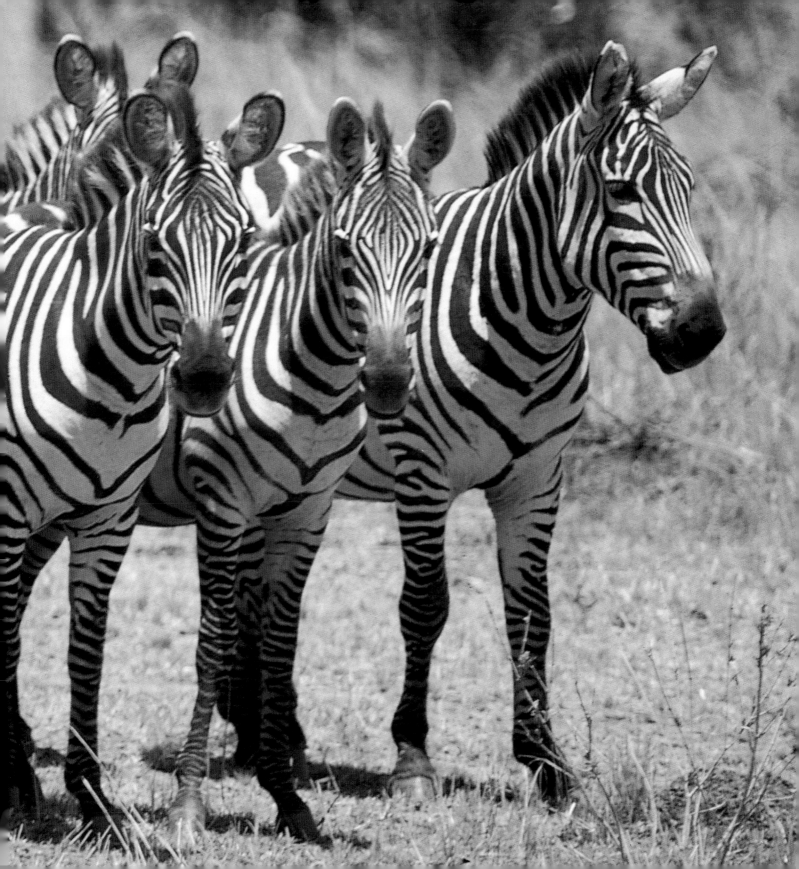

Zambia

Zambia, situated in southern Africa, consists mainly of plateaux situated between 1,000 and 1,500 metres above sea-level. These are home to a rich vegetation of Miombo forests, thornless deciduous woodland which starts its flowering cycle in August. Its fresh, red leaves then start to bathe the country in a single sea of colour that glows more strongly in the sunset after a hot day.

The fertile plains, the four mountains exceeding 2,000 metres that encourage mountain-hiking, the countless valleys and the Kalahari desert in the west of the country are major scenic attractions.

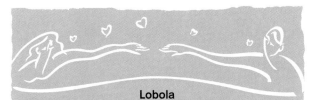

Lobola

In the past, marriages in Zambia were arranged mostly by the couple's parents; young people have more freedom in the choice of a partner nowadays. However, the elders are still consulted about most weddings and the lobola, the price for the bride is still negotiated. It is considered a sign of the bride's respect for her parents. In most tribes, the bride is brought to the groom's village on the eve of the wedding. Huge amounts of food are prepared and often beer is brewed specially for the wedding celebration. The entire village takes part in the festivities which last two or three days, as a rule. There is much singing, dancing and drumming during this period. When the celebration is over, the couple's parents prepare them for married-life by giving them pieces of advice. For instance, the bride is not allowed to cook until her parents-in-law have shown her how to the use the fireplace.

You can get to know old tribal cultures or discover the secrets of the rhinoceroses and other fascinating animals in the nature reserves.

Victoria Falls

A special highlight in Zambia are the breathtaking Victoria Falls about 300 kilometres west of Harare. Here the Zambesi River, at a width of nearly 1,700 metres, rushes down almost 110 metres into a gorge only about 50 metres wide. The spray from the waterfalls can splash up to a height of 400 metres and water the plants in a lush primeval forest directly nearby. The noise and mist from the plunging masses of water inspired the natives to name it "Mosi-oa-Tunya", which roughly means "smoke that dances" and which is wholly appropriate for the highly romantic place. What spot would be more suitable for a wedding-cum-honeymoon?

The Royal Livingstone*****

A unique natural experience
Victoria Falls/Livingstone

The first-class Sun International hotel bears the name of David Livingstone, the man who discovered the now famous waterfalls and christened them Victoria Falls, after the then Queen of England.

The reception-area of this "Leading Hotels of the World" is surrounded by a courtyard with fountains and steeped in the scent of the herb garden.
Guests can relax in the cosy seating unit on the lobby veranda, amidst decorative pillars, or select a book from the hotel library. Pictures in the lounge recall the exciting adventures of the Livingstones.

Accommodation & Amenities

Honeymooners who reside in the Royal Livingstone enjoy the view of the Zambesi River. The hotel has 173 en-suite rooms, three suites with a separate lounge and bedroom, as well as a President's Suite with two extra bedrooms. The two-storied Colonial manor-style villas, each with ten units that have their own veranda or terrace, breathe the elegance of a bygone era. Hand-woven carpets, pictures of animals, and the colour-scheme of green, cream and ivory create a splendid ambience. However, the rooms are dominated by African elements that remind the visitor that he is at one of the most historically-important places in Africa.

All of the rooms have individually-adjustable air-conditioning, satellite TV, radio and video, mini-safe and voice-mail-telephone. Room service is available and meals are served on one's own veranda if desired. However, the real highlight is a romantic dinner directly at the cliffs of the waterfalls.

Activities

You will find a gambling casino, several shopping opportunities, stands with local arts and crafts and a bicycle-rental in the entertainment centre "The Falls". It is possible to make safari trips both on land and water or to go fishing or horse-riding. Water-rafting, bungee-jumping, parachuting or climbing are available and you can book helicopter- or light aircraft-outings over the waterfalls or the Zambesi.

Honeymoon-extras/wedding

Honeymooners are given a room in the next highest category, depending on availability. Bridal couples are welcomed on arrival with fresh fruit, flowers, champagne and a gift. The first breakfast is served with champagne. You are taken by decorated car to the church ceremony in the hotel's festively decorated garden pavilion.

Services included

▸ Formalities for the civic wedding-ceremony in Livingstone City,
▸ including all permits and fees as well as the transfer
▸ A clergyman who marries all religious denominations
▸ Digital photographs of the ceremony
▸ E-mails to five friends
▸ A wedding-cake for ten people
▸ A bouquet for the bride and a lapel-flower for the groom
▸ Champagne and fruit for the wedding-night

Prices/addresses

A double-room with breakfast costs from £ 120 a night per person.

Sun International, Badgemore House, Gravel Hill,
Henley-on-Thames
GB Oxfordshire RG9 4NR, England
Tel: 01491-419-600
Fax: 01491-575-661

Kenya

Kenya, situated in eastern Africa on the coast of the Indian Ocean is famous for its wide variety of fauna. The large mammals that live in the savannahs, especially elephants, rhinoceroses, giraffes and zebras, attract many visitors each year to the 25 National Parks and 23 game reserves. The most famous is the Mount Kenya National Park which is on the World Heritage list.

Kenya has much more to offer, however. Divers, for example, find their paradise along its almost 500-kilometre-long coast with the Malindi Marine National Park and its numerous offshore coral-reefs. The ethnic and cultural diversity of the people is as rich as the variety of fauna. This becomes particularly clear when you travel from the centre of Swahili culture on the coast and go into the interior.

The climate, too, is one of strong contrasts. Although the country is situated on the level of the equator, the wide areas of Kenya's expansive plateaux have a moderate climate. Daytime temperatures are a pleasant 26° C even in the warmest months of January and February.

While the plateaux are characterised by grass savannahs with isolated acacias and papyrus forests, vast areas of the coast and the lowlands are covered by forests and brush. The dense rainforest on the country's southern and eastern mountainsides is outstanding here.

However, even the rainforest is only one of the natural wonders among Kenya's treasures. For instance, the country is divided from north to south by the East African Trench, an attraction which no visitor to Kenya should miss.

The many lakes of the country are also a striking nature-experience. Only a small part of one of the world's largest lakes, Lake Victoria, lies on Kenyan territory but Lake Turkana and Lake Nakuru are very worthwhile scenic attractions, too.

Governors' Ilmoran Camp****

An African dream comes true
Masai Mara

Dreaming of Out of Africa? Then shift your wedding or honeymoon to the Governors' Camp in the Masai Mara! The Masai Mara is undoubtedly one of the African game reserves best-known for a remarkable animal population.

Governors' Camp has been in existence since 1972. Africa's first permanent safari camp, Governors' Camp sets high standards featuring a close-to-nature, authentic safari on one hand, and comfort, service and outstanding cuisine on the other.

These qualities have become a tradition and the Camp has made a name for itself over the years. A special efford has been made to perserve the special atmosphere that inspired Hemingway and other world adventurers.

The new Governors' Ilmoran Camp – the most luxurious edition of the Governors' Camps – has been open since summer 2000 for people who do not wish to forego any comforts in the bush but still not miss the authentic, traditional safari feeling.

Accommodation & Amenities

The Governors' Ilmoran Camp, with only ten "suite-tents" along the Mara River, provides a particularly exclusive safari ambience and very personal service. From each tent, in the shade of centuries-old trees, you are able to enjoy not only the excellent view of the river with its rich wildlife but also your absolute privacy.

The interior decoration, with olive-wood furniture, textiles from the region and safari ornaments, contributes to the unique atmosphere in Ilmoran Camp. The en suite bathroom rounds off the camp's luxury. Each tent has its own spacious terrace with a fantastic unobstructed view.

Governors' Ilmoran Camp's public area has a restau-

rant- and bar-tent with a beautiful view of the river and a comfortable seating area decorated in traditional African style, where you may browse through inspiring books on Africa.

Ilmoran Camp cultivates the safari tradition of the evening campfire but private dinners, especially for wedding-guests, are willingly arranged on request. These can take place by candlelight on the tent's terrace or in the bush.

Activities

The game-rides in an open Land Rover, on which experienced guides bring you closer to the secrets of African wildlife, are very popular.

An equally exciting guided stalk on foot proceeds at a more leisurely pace. A safari in a hot-air balloon over the endless plains of the Masai Mara with a champagne bush-breakfast afterwards is another highlight.

It is worthwhile to visit one of the nearby Masai villages, the Masai school or the market for an insight into the culture of this nomadic tribe. To mark its 30th anniversary in 2002, the Governors' Ilmoran Camp has several packages for wedding-anniversaries and other special events.

A honeymoon trip to Mfangano Island Camp, the small tropical paradise on Lake Victoria, is highly recommendable. This dream-spot can be reached by a charter flight over the Masai Mara. The honeymoon suite there is out of this world – far form all civilisation, it is the perfect place to relax.

If you want to combine your honeymoon with a visit to another national park, you can start out from Lake Naivasha to the beautiful Loldia House, that also has a very beautiful setting.

Prices/addresses

A suite-tent in Governors' Ilmoran Camp is available for £ 540 per night, including full board, beverages (except for champagne and imported spirits), game-rides, a guided stalking tour on foot and laundry service.

Further information on Governors' Ilmoran Camp is available from:

Outposts: Nigel Crofton
Tel: 01647-23 10 07
Fax: 01647-23 10 08
e-mail: info@theoutposts.com

South Africa

Since the end of the apartheid policy, an ever-increasing number of tourists are discovering the South Africa sub-continent – a very special honeymoon destination, due to its great diversity. A combination with a stay on Mauritius or Seychelles is also ideal for a honeymoon trip.

The country, located on the southern tip of Africa between the Atlantic and the Indian Ocean, is characterized by an abundance of contrasts. For example, on the one hand there are the jagged peaks of the Drakensberg Mountains and, on the other, the fertile coastal region in the east, vast expanses with virtually endless horizons and a mysterious world of animals in the interior.

South Africa's seasons are exactly contrary to those in Europe. Clear differences exist between the moderate climate of the interior and the Mediterranean climate of the coasts. The climate in Natal, in the Kruger National Park and in North Transvaal can be even described as sub-tro-

Cattle for the bride

A wedding is a great community event among the Zulus, the largest ethnic group in South Africa. All residents of the district take part in the festivities. The older men sit comfortably in the shade drinking millet beer, warriors in full regalia display their skill in exhibition fights. Festively-dressed women and girls sing and dance in their respective age-groups. While the older women are dancing, the bride symbolically severs the ties to her past with a knife. She is now prepared to leave her own family and live with her husband's. The bridegroom had to pay the bride's father a price in the form of cattle or money before the wedding. This is to compensate her family for the non-availability of her labour and makes sure that she will be well-treated. She is allowed to keep the bridal price if she leaves her husband on grounds of cruelty.

pical. You can easily tour South Africa throughout the year but March to May and September/October are considered best. The winter months from May to September are particularly suitable for observing animals. Rainfall is heavier in the interior during the summer months and is more likely on the Western Cape during the South African winter. It can rain throughout the year on the southeastern coast.

Passenger flights to the country are available practically daily and last just three hours. There is no time lag.

A malaria vaccination is advisable for trips to the Kruger Park, Transvaal or Zululand. Similarly, you should use an insect repellent, especially in the evening-hours and at night. Further information is available from your family doctor.

Singita Private Game Reserve*****

Wildlife on the Sand River
Skukuza

The Singita Game Reserve is the perfect destination for honeymoon couples seeking excitement as well as romance. The exclusive lodge stands north of Skukuza in the Sabi Sand Game Reserve, a private wildlife reserve directly on the edge of the Kruger National Park.

In the South African Shangaan language, Singita means "wonder". This is an apt name in the light of the fascinating flora and fauna to be found in the 18,000-hectare reserve, which has remained completely unspoilt in part. Particularly its location in the middle of a magnificent hilly landscape with giant ebony-trees directly on the Sand River, makes the lodge a place with a very special flair. Those who dream of South Africa, dream of a place like this! The owner, Luke Nailes, also fulfilled a lifelong dream with this lodge that is a member of the renowned Relais & Chateaux group.

Accommodations & Amenities

Singita Game Reserve puts up visitors in the comfortable Ebony Lodge or in the Boulders Lodge that is equipped with every imaginable luxury. The latter holds first place in the rankings of the Relais & Chateau group on account of its special furnishings. The total 18 suites in both lodges are connected by wooden footbridges and all of them have a private swimming-pool. The generously-designed rooms each have a veranda, an open fireplace, lounge, bath, shower, toilet with an extra outdoor shower, air-conditioning, mini-bar, telephone, safe and hairdryer.

If you decide to stay in Boulders Lodge you can bathe not only in the pool but also in a free-standing bathtub with gold-plated legs. The total living area exceeds 200 square meters and has a panorama deck that compares to a huge terrace.

Singita Private Game Reserve
Sales & Marketing Office
P.O. Box 650881
Benmore 2010
South Africa
Tel: +27-11-234 09 90
Fax: +27-11-234 05 35

An open lounge, swimming-pool, terrace, bar and a souvenir shop are part of Singita Game Reserve. The restaurant boasts excellent cuisine and lays out the spread every evening in an open-air "boma", or traditional meeting-place. The culinary experience is rounded off by a drop of select wine from one of the 12,000 bottles in the wine-cellar.

Activities

You should not miss one of the game-rides that take place twice daily in an open cross-country vehicle, accompanied by experienced gamekeepers.

With some luck, you may even encounter the Big Five – elephants, lions, rhinoceroses, leopards and buffaloes – and other wild animals such as zebras, antelopes and giraffes. You can make direct contact with nature on walking-tours under the guidance of a ranger who knows his way around.

The hotel's private fitness-centre has all facilities for keeping your body in form.

Prices/address

Guests pay from about £ 440 per person for a night's stay in the Ebony Lodge or Boulders Lodge, with full board and two game-drives.

The Palace of The Lost City*****

An African fairy-tale castle
Sun City

Every year, more than three million guests from all over the world visit Sun City, an international holiday resort featuring an African theme park that opened in 1992: "The Lost City". The Sun International Resort is located 187 kilometers away from Johannesburg next to the Pilanesberg National Park. The Palace, flagship ot the area including three other Hotels, was finished in April 1998 and is a member of the "Leading Hotels of the World".

The Palace of the Lost City is in the middle of a tropical rainforest, that was planted especially for the hotel resort. The luxury hotel is supposedly based on the royal residence of an imaginary African King. However the eight towers and the giant cupola above the entrance hall are are much more reminiscent of the palace of an Indian maharadscha. Only precious materials were chosen for the building and furniture, such as cristall, marble and other valuable materials and timbers. The entrance hall is decorated with archs that are formed by elephant tusks of imitation ivory, bronze balustrades and jungle areas. This lavish splendour is spread all over the 338 luxury suites and rooms.

Accommodation & Amenities

The extremely luxurious and generously laid-out rooms and suites with a view of the marine park or the hotel's private golf-course have a bath/shower, telephone, air-conditioning, radio, mini-bar, TV/video, hairdryer, safe and 24-hour service. The Royal Suite is the highlight of the hotel and is one of the world's most beautiful hotel-rooms.

Enjoy the inimitable atmosphere in the two excellent a la carte restaurants or in the palm-lounge!

Artificial rivers and fountains flow into ponds of sea-roses and palm-skirted pools. The Bridge of Time, a multi-visual show about the legend of a sunken kingdom at this spot, is also part of this almost storybook world of experiences.

Activities

The marine park, Valley of the Waves, is a challenge even to experienced surfers with its artificially-created waves. It is nestled in the jungle-like landscape. Jet-skiing, para-sailing and windsurfing are also on the programme. Golfers, including world-class professionals, are attracted to the Gary Player Country Club in Sun City. This has been the venue of the world's highest-paid competition for years now. A further 18-hole course has been built for less-experienced players in the meantime.

Minigolf, horse-riding, 11 tennis courts, a fitness centre, squash courts and a bowling-alley are also available to active sportsmen. You can recuperate for hours in the sauna or the massage suite. Fans of top-flight entertainment will get their money's worth in the Superbowl concert-hall. It is housed in the entertainment centre together with the gaming casinos.

Safaris and balloon-trips and other events are organized regularly in the neighbouring 35,000-hectare Pilanesberg National Park.

Honeymoon extras/wedding

You can tie the knot in the Palace too. A romantic wedding-chapel was built specially for this purpose. Together

with the exotic garden against the backdrop of Pilanesberg, it is the perfect setting for a wedding ceremony. Sun City takes care of everything neccessary to make the big day an unforgettable event, starting from the floral decorations and the wedding-cake and extending to the banqueting arrangements with special wedding menus.

Prices/addresses

A night, including breakfast, costs from about £ 125 per person in a Standard room, in a Deluxe room from £ 140 per person and in the Royal Suite £ 530 per person.

The Palace of the Lost City (Sun International)
P.O. Box 3, Sun City 0316
South Africa
Tel: +27-14 55-731 31
Fax: +27-14 55-732 30

Sun International UK
Tel: +44-(0)1491-419-600
Fax: +44-(0)1491-575-661

INDIAN OCEAN

Seychelles

Seen from an aircraft, the mountain-peaks on Seychelles resemble cones that have accidentally fallen into the water. One can just make out the reefs surrounding the islands, below the sparkling sea-surface. As the plane approaches, the green palm-groves, brilliant-grey granite cliffs and white beaches that make each of the isles a paradise become recognizable.

The archipelago consists of 92 islands with a total area of 454 square kilometres; it is situated 1,600 kilometres from Mombasa, Kenya, and four kilometres south of the equator. The local population is able to look back on French, British, Indian, Chinese, Arab and African ancestry. Perhaps this cultural diversity is the source of the friendliness and warmth with which the people of Seychelles approach tourists.

The flora and fauna are unique. A wide variety of endemic species can still be found on the islands. With luck it is possible to encounter a giant turtle out in the open. The most famous fruit is coco de mer, the sea-coconut whose curves involuntarily reflect the human female form.

Legend has it that the unusually-shaped nut is the ultimate proof that Seychelles is where Eve seduced Adam with an apple. This create the perfect atmosphere for this group of islands in the Indian ocean as the ideal honeymoon destination.

When leaving the hotel premises on occasion, you will be surprised at how quiet it is away from the tourist resorts. Whether on secluded beaches or in the centre of town, lovers will have no problem finding undisturbed, romantic spots.

Temperatures on Seychelles are between 21° and 30° C throughout the year; humidity is 80 per cent. Rainfall is somewhat higher from November to March because of the northwestern monsoon but there is neither a distinct rainy season nor violent storms. Only a nine-hour flight separates Central Europe from paradise.
Seychelles is thus ideal for honeymooners who have only a few days free but nevertheless do not want to miss the seclution of the magnificent white beaches and tropical paradise.

Romantic Wedding Praslin

There are a large number of romantic places for weddings on Mahe, Praslin and La Digue: for example, the terrace of a Colonial-style house on Mahe or the famous cliffs of the Anse Source d'Argent bay on La Digue.

The Fisherman's Wharf at Hotel Coco de Mer on Praslin and the luxurious catamaran Charming Lady are also extremely popular with bridal couples.

What deadlines are to be observed?
Provided that all necessary documents are with the travel operator at least four weeks before takeoff, marriages are possible on the first working day after arrival, even on Saturday for a small extra charge.

What documents are necessary?
▶ Passport and certified Birth Certificates mentioning the place of birth
▶ Certificate of spouse's death if widowed (certified by a registrar)

▶ Short form of final divorce certificate, if divorced

Services included
▶ Wedding-ceremony on the decorated pier of Fisherman's Wharf or on the Charming Lady
▶ Wedding address by a registrar
▶ witnesses
▶ Wedding-cake and champagne at the ceremony
▶ Photographer plus 36 pictures and negatives
▶ Orchids for the bride, a lapel-flower for the groom
▶ Assistance with the registration and certification of the marriage, all fees

Price per couple from about £ 690

Half-day rental for the Charming Lady about £ 610

Little (or no) brides
A wedding on Seychelles is traditionally a huge celebration and a very expensive affair. Perhaps, this is due to the fact that many of the islanders, although Catholic, do without a church or civic wedding-ceremony. Those wishing to start a family move in with their partner; however there are also many single mothers on this island. Instead of a wedding celebration, the first Holy Communion is now the most important day for many women. Each girl attends church on this day clad like a bride in a dress of white lace and with a tulle-veil.

Hotels Coco de Mer****
& Black Parrot*****

In the kingdom of the giant coconut
Praslin

Praslin is the second largest of the inner Seychelles islands and can be reached several times daily by a 15-minute flight from Mahe international airport. A visit to the island is rewarding if only because of the Vallee de Mai, a unique nature reserve. Well-tended trails take you through untouched vegetation. The nature-park in the eastern part of the island was opened about 40 years ago to protect the last 4,000 palms that bear the giant sea coconuts (coco de mer). Many legends surround the oddly-shaped giant nuts, creating the myth that they act as an aphrodisiac. Bird-lovers will be delighted by the black parrots, a rare species which, like the bulbul and the blue pigeon, are at home here.

The Coco de Mer Hotel and the neighbouring all suite-hotel Black Parrot, named after Praslin's flora- and fauna attractions, are in a secluded area at one of the island's most beautiful spots, surrounded by a large nature park with tropical flora and fauna.

From here you can visit Praslin's northern region, where the hiking trails lead to the beautiful Anse Georgette and Petite Anse Kerlan, the snorkelling paradise.

Accommodation & Amenities

40 comfortable chalet styled rooms nestled in a skilfully laid-out ocean-view garden. All of them have a large four poster bed, corner seating unit, safe, bath/shower and toilet, air conditioning and ceiling-fans, satellite-TV, mini-refrigerator, telephone and veranda.

A restaurant, boutique and the reception area are located in the main building.

The Hibiscus Restaurant, provides a lavish buffet in the morning, a delicious choice menu is served four evenings a week while a large buffet is set up for the duration of the three nights. Creole grilled dishes are its speciality.

You also enjoy a fantastic view of the beach and sea from the suites of the Black Parrot. Twelve luxurious suites 60 to 80 square metres in size (photo shows the Junior Suite) are furnished with corner seating units, balconies and full ameneties ensuring perfect comfort. The hotel has its own restaurant, swimming-pool, bar and reception area.

Activities

As well as the swimming-pool in the shape of a sea-coconut, a wide range of sporting activities such as table-tennis tables, one squash court, tennis courts, windsurfers, canoes and a separate children's pool are available for use at no extra cost.

You may hire diving-masks, snorkels and bicycles for a small fee. Similarly, boat-trips for deep-sea fishing, and guided nature-study tours through the Vallee de Mai are on the programme for a fee. There is also a golf course nearby.

Honeymoon extras

The friendly hotel staff welcome honeymooners with flowers and sparkling wine.

Reserve the garden pavilion on the terrace of the Black Parrot suites for a romantic dinner during your honeymoon.

Prices/addresses

Accommodation in Hotel Coco de Mer costs from around £ 62 per person and night, including breakfast, and from about £ 83 with half-board.

The Black Parrot suites with half-board are from around £ 110 per person and night.

Hotel Coco de Mer
Anse Bois de Rose
Praslin
Seychelles
Tel: +248-23 39 00
Fax: +248-23 39 19

Acajou****

An island paradise with endless white beaches
Cote d'Or, Praslin

Some of the most wonderful beaches in Seychelles are on the island of Praslin. The Hotel Acajou, named after this beautiful, precious hardwood, stands directly on one of them. The family-owned complex is personally supervised by Joanise Doway.

Accommodation & Amenities
Only natural materials such as mahogany were used to design the 28 rooms, giving them a tropical flair.
The well-furnished, spacious rooms are in two wings of the building and surrounded by luxuriant takamaka and casuarina trees. Each room has a bath and shower. Standard conveniences include air-conditioning, TV, ISDN-telephone, radio and mini-bar. In addition, four Superior rooms at the very front of the hotel provide individual safes, tea and coffee making facilities as well.

The hotel-pool invites one to relax and the beach-bar stocks refreshing accompanying drinks.

Gourmets will be delighted with the exquisite delicacies that are featured on the hotel's restaurant-menu. The cocktail lounge entices with tropical delights in the evening and the bar with a choice of classical drinks. The evening programme features light entertainment or you can enjoy the mild evenings on your private ocean-view balcony.

Activities
A diving centre that can be used for a fee is located very near to the hotel-complex. The hotel makes bookings there on request. Bicycles may be hired nearby to explore the island as you wish and you should not miss out on an outing to the beautiful Coco-de-Mer Valley.

An elegant gambling-casino in which you can try your luck is within walking distance from Hotel Acajou. You can also experience the variety of life on the neighbouring island of La Digue. The landing-stage for the boats to the island is just ten minutes away by taxi.

Services included

▶ Marriage ceremony on the beach,
  including organisation
▶ witnesses and a registrar
▶ Photographer
▶ Assistance with the formalities: Registration and
  certification of the wedding
▶ Festive decoration with flowers
▶ Wedding-cake and champagne

Price per couple from about £ 630

Prices/addresses

A night in a standard-room with half-board costs from about £ 85 per person.

Hotel Acajou
Cote d'Or, Praslin
Seychelles
Tel: +248-23 24 00
Fax: +248-23 24 01
e-mail: acajou@seychelles.net
www.seychelles.net/acajou

Lémuria Resort of Praslin******

A dream of island-life
Anse Kerlan, Praslin

There is a large piece of land in the north-western part of
Praslin island which, legend says, was left over from Paradise when the continents separated millions of years ago.
This is the Lemuria Resort, a Constance Hotel and member of the Relais & Chateaux Hotels. A fantastic variety of
flora and fauna, turquoise-blue water and three fine sandy beaches - the very quiet Grande Anse Kerlan, the Petite Anse Kerlan with the watersports centre and the secluded Anse Georgette - await visitors just 10 minutes away
from Praslin's airstrip. The hotel is nestled among tropical
gardens and characterised by tasteful elegance. It is the
perfect place for relaxation and a memorable setting for
the most wonderful day in one's life.

Accommodation & Amenities
The hotel has 88 luxurious and individually-designed
Junior Suites (52 square meters), eight Senior Suites (115
square meters) with a separate living-room and lounge,
eight new poolside villas (725 square meters) and a Presi-
dential Villa (1,250 square meters) with a private swim-

ming pool and butler-service on request. All of the suites have a terrace or balcony with a limited sea-view. There is a choice between four exclusive bars and three restaurants; the Seahorse which serves classical Mediterranean cuisine, the Beach Restaurant where refreshing seafood and salads are available and The Legend which brings international specialities to the table.

Activities

The area features a fitness centre, a sauna with cold plunge pool, Jacuzzi, steam-bath and a Guerlain institute offering a variety of massages and body treatments. Guests may use the first and only hotel-owned 18-hole golf-course on Seychelles for a green-fee. Sailing, windsurfing, kayak, catamaran- and pedalo-rides as well as snorkelling are available to water-sport enthusiasts. Diving, deep sea fishing and cycling are also possible on a fee paying basis. You can also sign up for sports lessons.

Honeymoon extras/wedding

A 25 per cent bridal discount is valid from May 1 to July 31 and September 1 to October 31 as from 2003. Each couple is presented with a basket of fruit and a bottle of French champagne on arrival as well as a romantic candlelight dinner – excluding drinks – that is served in the suite during the stay.

Prices/addresses

A night in a Junior Suite costs from £ 170 per person with breakfast.

Reservations:
Infinity Specialist Tours Ltd.
Tel: 01491-57 15 45
Fax: 01491-63 61 59
e-mail: info@infinitytours.co.uk

Alphonse Island Lodge****

A divers' paradise
Alphonse Island

The 172-hectare triangular coral-island Alphonse Island lies 450 kilometres south of Mahe. Its coastline is 3.6 kilometres long and stretches around a turquoise-coloured lagoon protected by a reef.

You can walk around the island along small paths in about one-and-a-half hours and gain an insight into the tropical vegetation. It includes papaws, bananas, cotton and sisal which was planted on the island in the 19th century and processed into thread for sacks and bags.

Shipwrecks on the seabed of the island's two pointed foothills are ideal for outings.
On one side of the island, the remnants of the French steamship Doile, which sank on the way to Reunion in

November 1873, can be explored at low tide, which is quite an adventurous tour.

The Tamatave which ran aground on the other side 30 years later is one of the island's diving-spots today. The Abyss, a site with black coral, an intact coral reef and a variety of underwater fauna, including sea-turtles, sharks and parrot-fish is a source of fascination for divers.

The island was opened to tourists in spring of 2000. They can select between one of the 25 bungalows or one of the five Deluxe Villas. While the South African designer Florence Masson chose a rather typical island-style for the bungalows – on stilts and with a thatched roof –

the ground-level Deluxe Villas are in more of a modern bungalow-style. All holiday lodgings stand on the edge of the lagoon, nestled in tropical vegetation. An extensive coconut-palm forest borders the lodge.

Accommodation & Amenities

The rooms are very spacious and equipped with electric-fans and air-conditioning. All bungalows and villas have a veranda that provides an incomparable view at any time of day.

Each bungalow has a queen-sized bed, a large bathroom with Jacuzzi-tub and an open-air shower which, naturally, is built to ensure privacy.

Holidaymakers are given full board in the excellent island-restaurant; the menu is based mainly on the daily fishing catch and fresh vegetables from the island-farm.

Activities

Rental of water-sports equipment such as canoes, surfboards, and snorkelling-gear are included in the price, as are bicycles.

Diving with professional services and trips to the neighbouring islands of Bijoutier and Saint Francois, two of the top locations for tropical fly-fishing, are offered for a fee.

Honeymoon-extra

The honeymoon offer is valid from mid-January to the end of November. With a minimum stay of five nights, it includes a free flight for the bride and a special dinner with a bottle of champagne.

Prices/addresses

A night costs about £ 220 per person including full board. The flight to Mahe, the main island, costs about £ 190 per person.

Alphonse Island Lodge
P.O. Box 1273
Victoria, Seychelles
Tel: +248-22 90 30
Fax: +248-22 90 34

Frégate Island Private******

A honeymoon "beyond the world"
Frégate

A 19th century British governor described Seychelles as being "1,000 miles beyond the world". Even today, guests on Fregate Island, way in the east of the island group, feel far away from stress, everyday hustle and bustle, and mass tourism. Although Fregate Island is just about 60 kilometres from Mahe airport, only a few tourists find their way to the island paradise.

It would be better to steer clear of Fregate Island if you are looking for active nightlife. Instead, the island of about three square kilometres in area, has seven fantastic beaches, crystal-clear water, extensive coral reefs, sun, and flora and fauna that are rich in endemic species.

Sixteen exclusive luxurious villas, directly bordered by the small idyllic bay Anse Ramou with its snow-white coral beach, are available to the island's visitors.

Grand Anse in the island's south-west is another sandy beach that is particularly well-suited for snorkelling and diving.

West of the complex of villas is the impressive Anse Victorin, with one of the world's most beautiful beaches; the powdery sand is interspersed with typical granite rocks.

Accommodation & Amenities
The 16 villas decorated by the renowned American interior designers Wilson & Associates harmonise well with their surroundings and are arranged so that they afford absolute privacy, even from the closest neighbours.

Two of the villas were built for families on coveted meadows, all others stand above the steep coast. You have a magnificent sea-view from all of the holiday homes. Each of these almost 180-square-metres architectural masterpieces has a bedroom (with a large bath and toilet) and a living room (with shower and toilet) housed in separate bungalows. A roofed terrace links the two areas. A private Jacuzzi, a king-sized daybed, carved wooden sunbeds and a covered dining area are on the large sundeck.

The villas, textured with warm shades of wood and with pointed thatched roofs of Indonesian grass, are perfectly integrated into the tropical garden that surrounds the complex. Each of these sanctuaries is fully glassed-in on

the ocean-side and therefore gives you an unobstructed view of the ocean and the lush vegetation.

The walls and furniture are of hand-carved woods, the upholstery covered with Thai silk and Egyptian cotton. Antiques and pieces of art from Singapore, Thailand, Indonesia and Myanmar lend each villa a personal note, the cleverly-placed lighting steeps the rooms in a home-ly glow.

Technical comforts such as air-conditioning, cassette- and video recorders, CD- and DVD-players as well as a private house-bar are also included. Telephone and fax are available to guests who do not want to be cut off from the outer world, even in paradise. Discreet service ensures that fresh flowers and fruit are in the rooms every morning.

The restaurant in the main building spoils you not only with outstanding international cuisine but also with a splendid view of the Indian Ocean. Gourmets may enjoy the Creole cuisine in the historic Plantation House, a renovated mansion from the Colonial era, which now houses the island's museum.

If you prefer to eat in the privacy of your own villa, then naturally use can be made of the 24-hour room-service. The restaurants are supplied with home-grown fruit and vegetables from the island's private farm, thus guarante-eing absolutely fresh ingredients.

Activities
A small gym, a library with a wide choice of literature, DVDs and CDs as well as a playing area for children are located in the centre of the complex. A seawater pool of unusual design was built into a cliff. Guided hikes aro-und the island and mountain-bikes are provided for free. There is a charge for manicures, pedicures and massages.

The range of water-sports on Fregate Island (Private) is superb. The resort has a small fleet of yachts and speed-boats for fishing trips and sunset cruises. The outings into the underwater world of the coral reefs are a high-light for every diver. The resort requests a fee for this. Non-motorised water-sports are included in the room-price. Those who prefer firm ground under their feet are able to take long strolls through the shady hiking trails that lead all over the island.

Prices/addresses
A villa on Fregate Island is available from about £ 1,400 per night including full board and all non-alcoholic beverages.

Reservations:
Infinity Specialist Tours Ltd.
Tel: 01491-57 15 45
Fax: 01491-63 61 59
e-mail: info@infinitytours.co.uk

Banyan Tree******

Island Paradise
Mahe

Mahe, with an area of 150 square miles, is the largest of the Seychelles islands and has the highest mountain, the Morne Seychelles rising to 2969 feet above sea level. A great place to spend an active holiday, especially mountain-climbing. However, the island has many other attractions to offer.

In the north, the world's smallest capital city, Victoria, extends a welcome invitation to visitors. The hustle and bustle of the fish and vegetable markets are a must, as are the Victoria Clock Tower and the colourful wooden buildings from the turn of the century.

There are mountains in the south of the island, which offer a tranquil and unspoiled environment. Here you can wander through lush forests, discover fascinating flora and fauna, and laze on powdery, endless white sand beaches.

Banyan Tree is the newest Seychelles resort and the highest-quality hotel on the whole of Mahe Island. Nestled in a bay with a spectacular view of the Indian Ocean, surrounded by coconut palms and tropical forests, the resort is top among the latest generation of luxury hotels on the Seychelles Islands. Spoil yourselves with indulgent opulena!

Accommodation & Amenities
The hotel consists of 15 luxurious beach-villas and 20 comfortable villas on the slopes, surrounded by lush vegetation.

Each villa has its own pool and garden; all beach-villas have a pavilion containing two massage-beds and a whirlpool. Bridal couples can enjoy their own company in total privacy, the staff will prepare and serve all meals in the villas if guests so choose.

Each romantic villa is decorated with works by local artists specially created for the ambience.

Then there is the President's Villa. It is situated on a small separate bay and has two pools, two sun-terraces, two bedrooms, dressing rooms, an open-air Jacuzzi, outside-showers, as well as an extra living and dining-pavilion. Immerse yourself in the impressive landscape and allow yourself to be inspired by the captivating magic of this Villa.

In addition, a beauty-parlour, various bars and restaurants are available. Try the Creole delicacies in the restaurant Au Jardin d' Epices, in La Varangue or in Saffron, where you can allow skilfully-spiced coconut- and curry-dishes for which Seychelles is renowned, to melt in your mouth!

Activities

There is a wide range of sports activities on offer, such as canoe- and kayak outings, table-tennis, volleyball or windsurfing. You may relax in the fitness-centre or join in yoga- and meditation courses.

Honeymoon extras

The wedding ceremony takes place on the terrace of an old Colonial house in a nearby local artists' colony. The honeymooners are welcomed with a bottle of wine and a basket of tropical fruit on arrival.

Prices/addresses

Accommodation in a Hillside-Pool-Villa costs from £ 240 per person per night with breakfast.

Banyan Tree Seychelles
Anse Intendance, Mahe
Republic of Seychelles
Tel: +248-38 35 00
Fax: +248-38 36 00

Wedding-package "Creole Wedding"

What arrangements are needed?
Marriage is possible a few days after arrival (but only Mondays to Fridays), provided that all necessary documents have reached Infinity at least six weeks before takeoff.

What documents are necessary?
▶ Passport copies and birth certificates mentioning also place of birth
▶ Certificate of spouse's death if widowed
▶ Short form of final divorce certificate, if divorced.

Services included
▶ Transfer from the airport to the hotel
▶ Wedding ceremony on the terrace of a Colonial-style house in a small artists' colony
▶ Wedding-cake and champagne
▶ A romantic wedding-meal
▶ A bouquet of flowers for the bride, a lapel-flower for the groom
▶ Musical accompaniment by a solo musician
▶ Assistance with the registration and certification of the marriage, all liable fees

Price per couple about £ 800

Air Seychelles

Seychelles, with a population of nearly 80,000, is probably the smallest country in the world that operates its own airline. Nevertheless, despite the small domestic market, Air Seychelles has prevailed internationally against the major airline companies. This is due, not least of all, to a service organised to meet the wishes and needs of its passengers.

The national airline was established at the end of the 1970s and has been making regular international flights since 1983 for which it uses two modern Boeing 767-300 ER planes. These models are statistically among the world's safest and most reliable aircraft. Incidentally, the average age of the fleet is only 2.5 years. Pilots with many years experienced fly the passengers safely to their destinations.

The flight crew are mostly Seychellois and reflect the ethnic diversity of their homeland. They spoil the passengers with the generous charm and the well-known heartiness of the local population.

The network of routes is impressive. The airline flies to 14 destinations on three continents each week - London (Gatwick), Paris (Charles de Gaulle), Rome, Zurich, Johannesburg, Singapore, Dubai, Munich, Frankfurt, Milan, Mauritius, Reunion, The Maldives and The Comoro Archipelago.

A Boeing 767 flies twice a week from Gatwick to the international airport that was opened in 1971 in Victoria, the Seychelles capital.

Air Seychelles seeks close co-operation with other airlines wherever possible, mostly in joint ventures. The Seychelles and Mauritius entered such an alliance in 1997 which led to stronger co-operation within the region and to a considerable expansion of the flight connections between the two popular destinations in the Indian Ocean. The airline can also be proud of its on-board services. The popular Pearl Class, a combination of First- and Business Class, affords 24 passengers a lot of comfort on long-distance flights in armchairs arranged in pairs. The space between seats – 50 inches – ensures generous legroom.

The culinary care provided by Air Seychelles in all classes is also internationally recognised. The airline attaches special importance to the regional Creole cuisine – always combined with the international quality supply – in keeping with the motto Flying in the Creole Spirit.

The friendliness and cordial smile of the cabin crew do the rest to put the passengers in the mood for the approaching holiday.

On Seychelles itself, the island connections are handled by four 20-seater DeHavilland Twin Otter DHC6 aircraft. A rapid, reliable service links the six main islands of the

Seychelles Archipelago, Mahe, Praslin, Bird, Denis, Fregate and Desroches, with each other.
Long-distance passengers flying with Air Seychelles from Europe get a special rate for the connecting flight from Mahe to Praslin. Naturally, this island-hopping can be booked at the same time as the trip.

Prices/addresses
Air Seychelles flies each Friday and Sunday from Gatwick directly to Mahe. The flight costs from about £ 690 per person in the Economy Class, including taxes.

Air Seychelles
Oak Cottage
County Oak Way, Crawley
West Sussex, RH11 7ST
Tel. +44-1293-59 66 55
Fax. +44-1293-59 66 58
www.airseychelles.co.uk

Mauritius

"Mauritius was created first. Heaven was created after. Heaven was copied from Mauritius."
(Mark Twain in Following the Equator)

Mauritius, the divine island about 3,000 kilometres off the eastern African coast, is one of contrasts. Snow-white, far-stretching beaches line deep-blue lagoons, green sugarcane plantations cover the plains at the foot of the black hills and avenues of flamboyant trees glow flaming-red in front of white Colonial-style villas nestled in well-tended palm-gardens. The tropical rainforest in the south-west and the famous coral gardens on the coast are other scenic highlights. More than a million people live on Mauritius, a colourful mixture of Indians, Creoles, Chinese and Europeans that have left their mark on the island's culture.

Many factors speak for Mauritius. The island can be reached by air in about eleven hours and the time difference is just two to three hours so no sluggish jetlag develops. Trade winds ensure pleasant beach-weather all year round. Air temperature averages 24° C in winter (Jun-Aug) and 31° C in summer (Nov-Feb). Heavy rainstorms can occur in December and January but usually they are brief. Water temperatures are between 22 and 27° C. Neither a visa nor vaccinations are required for entry and communication in English is easy throughout the country. Despite the ever-growing number of visitors, Mauritius has remained free of mass tourism to a large extent. Therefore, the population's honest hospitality can be felt everywhere, not least of all in the service of the many wonderful hotels of every category.

Therefore, it is no wonder that the island is among the most popular destinations for newlyweds. Many hotels offer high bridal discounts and honeymoon extras between May and September. The national airline, Air Mauritius, even grants honeymooners special fares and preferential service during this period. Thanks to the island's scenic and cultural diversity, the most varied possibilities exist for organizing weddings there.

The walk around the fire
A Hindu wedding traditionally lasts for four days filled with rituals to strengthen the relationship between bride and groom.
The actual marriage ceremony takes place on the third day. A priest opens the ceremony with prayers in Sanskrit. Bride and groom, both decorated with garlands of flowers, sit in front of a fire and offer it diffrent sacrifices. Both then walk around the holy fire four times, touching a stone each time.
This symbolises future obstacles in their life, which they intend to overcome jointly. Before they take seven further steps around the fire, the bridegroom places a cotton string with various pendants around his future wife's neck. The knotting of this string is the highlight of the ceremony.
Finally, the groom marks a spot above the base of his wife's nose with red powder (bindi), which is supposed to open her "third eye".

Paradise Wedding

Just one look at the snow-white beaches, the lagoons and the turquoise-coloured ocean and you're sure to get into a special honeymoon mood. What's more, this is an ideal place where wedding vows can be exchanged.

It is not only the excellent hotels and the magnificent landscape that form a wonderful setting for "the most beautiful day in one's life". If you wish a religious ceremony, you can marry either in a Roman Catholic or Protestant (Presbyterian) Church, or according to Hindu or Buddhist rites. No matter what rites you choose, everyone – from the decorator to the pastry-maker – does his best to make your wedding-day unforgettable.

Still can't decide? Then simply marry according to four different rites. Your wedding-day timetable could then look like this:

About ten o'clock in the morning, the civil ceremony on the private beach of the hotel Sugar Beach Resort, cutting of the wedding-cake and a toast with a glass of champagne.

About one p.m., exchanging rings in the Presbyterian Church in Phoenix. On to a Buddhist temple in Port Louis for the third vow.

The Hindu ceremony follows in the late afternoon. Bride and groom are dressed in the traditional wedding-robes and decorated with garlands of flowers.

The evening is rounded off with a candlelight dinner to the accompaniment of a traditional sega band.

What deadlines are to be observed?

In principle, a wedding-ceremony can be performed two working days after arrival on Mauritius, provided that all documents have been received by the travel operator at least six weeks before takeoff. However a minimum stay of five nights is recommended in order to ensure smooth processing.

What documents are necessary?

Provided that the wedding is booked with a tour operator:
- Passport copies (valid for at least six months on arrival) and certified or original birth certificates mentioning the place of birth
- Form: Application to Marry for Non-citizens (obtainable from the tour operator)
- If divorced or widowed: Certificate of divorce or death certificate of the deceased partner.
- If the Bride is divorced less than 300 days, a negative local pregnancy test is required
- For minors: A notarised sworn translation of consent by the parents or legal guardian

For a church-wedding:
- Informal declaration of agreement by the local parish with a referral to the Presbyterian Church in Mauritius
- For Catholics: Form "Referral for Marriage Abroad" from the local parish with certification by the Seat of the diocese

EXAMPLE FOR A WEDDING ARRANGEMENT ON MAURITIUS:

"Paradise Wedding Mauritius"
Services included:

- 5 nights/half-board in a comfortable beach-hotel
- Private transfer airport-hotel-airport
- Wedding-ceremony at a specially decorated venue on the beach or in the hotel-area
- Wedding-cake and champagne
- Photographer for souvenir pictures (including photos and negatives)
- Bridal bouquet
- Assistance with registration and certification of the marriage
- All local fees
From about £ 1,210 per couple

The following bookings can be made additionally:

- Video/PAL from about £ 170
- Romantic candlelight dinner from about £ 35
- Sega folklore entertainment or a trio from about £ 205
- Wedding-ceremony in a romantic chalet in the central mountain range with a view of the south coast and the Morne Brabant (including transfer, wedding-meal and two musicians) from about £ 170 per couple
- Anglican or Catholic wedding in the church (including transfer)
- floral decorations in the church and an obligatory donation from about £ 170 per couple
- Hindu or Buddhist ceremony (including transfer, blessing, donation to the temple, rental charge for the traditional robes) about £ 170 per couple

Hotel Sugar Beach Resort*****

Manor House and villas in the tropical garden
Flic en Flac, West Coast

The Hotel Sugar Beach Resort, a reasonably-priced dream for honeymooners, is nestled among breathtakingly beautiful garden complexes directly on a long beach of powdery sand. The romantic architecture of the villas takes you back to the Colonial era. A special feature is the giant swimming-pool where dinner is served in the evening.

Accommodation & Amenities
There are 238 pleasantly-furnished rooms fitted with bath/toilet, air-conditioning, TV and video-recorder, mini-bar, telephone, safe and hairdryer. The rooms have their own terrace and are located in groups of ten among the garden-villas and the Manor House.

All of the rooms face the sea and the beach-villas have a direct sea-view. Apart from the giant swimming-pool with

bar, there are four restaurants and snack-bars in the garden as well as a tea-garden in which five o'clock tea is celebrated Colonial-style.

Activities
The use of the tennis courts, gym, kayaks, mini-sailing and paddle boats are all part of the complimentary recreational package, as is windsurfing, snorkelling, water-skiing and participation in outings with the glass bottomed boat. Deep-sea fishing, parasailing, mountain-biking and diving are available for a fee.

Honeymoon-extras
Bridal couples recieve a 25 per cent discount per person off the already reasonable off-season prices between May and mid-October. Flowers and fruit, a pareo, a T-shirt and a special seafood dinner on one evening await all honeymooners on arrival.

Prices/addresses
The stay costs from about £ 60 per person per night with half-board.

Hotel Sugar Beach Resort
Wolmar, Flic en Flac
Mauritius
Tel: +230-453 90 90
Fax: +230-453 91 00

Dinarobin*****

A paradise for peace and tranquility
Le Morne Peninsula, Southwest Coast

This exclusive all-suite resort of the Beachcomber chain was opened in 2001 on the Mauritian southwestern coast. Bridal couples are able to take a break from everyday routines and explore the 1,200-square-metre oasis at the foot of Le Morne mountain. The oriental-style courtyards and the palm-bordered swimming pool transport you into another world, providing the necessary peace and composure for a tranquil stay.

There are more than 170 suites in thatch-roofed, local-style bungalows that line the flawless beaches of the sea-washed peninsula, which are available as honeymoon homes.

Accommodation & Amenities

The 148 Junior Suites feature a small anteroom, seating unit, bedroom and bathroom, total area of about 65 square meters in size and all available with a balcony or terrace. The 24 Senior Suites with an area of about 115 square metres have separate living-and bedrooms. The culinary range in Dinarobin is wide and rich in variety: Here you can feast on Chinese, Creole, Indian, Italian or other international dishes. A host of gourmet delights await you in one of the four top restaurants in the neighbouring Le Paradis hotel.

Activities

Honeymooners are spoilt with numerous wellness programmes in the luxurious spa. Oriental patios, quiet gardens, mosaics and fountains all combine to create an Arabian Nights atmosphere. Six rooms are provided for treatments ranging from foot reflex-zone massage to acupressure. Two hydrotherapy rooms, two algotherapy rooms, and two Finnish saunas are additional possible options for easy relaxation. If you prefer an activity holiday, you can select from a wide range of aquatic sports including water-skiing, windsurfing, sailing, snorkelling, kayaking or pedalo-trips. Paid water sports include diving or deep-

sea fishing. An outing with the glass-bottomed boat opens up the region's wonderful undersea world even to the water-shy.

Land sports which are subject to a fee include tennis, golf on the 18-hole course and mountain bike expeditions around the island. The facilities of the Paradis Hotel are also available to the guests and offer even greater variety.

Honeymoon extras

A honeymoon discount of 25 per cent is granted, except from December 20 to January 8. The couples are greeted with a seafood candlelight-dinner, champagne and a bowl of fresh tropical fruit in their room and also two T-shirts.

Prices/addresses

Accommodation in a Junior Suite costs from about £ 120 per person and night.

Dinarobin, Hotel Golf & Spa
Le Morne Peninsula,
Mauritius
Tel: +230-401 49 00
Fax: +230-401 49 01

Legends****

Feng-Shui oasis for honeymooners
Grand Gaube, Grand Bay

This exclusive hotel is located in the north-west of the island of Mauritius in the famous Grand Bay. The modern, luxurious complex is located directly on a dream beach that attracts swimmers and sunbathers. The special feature of this hotel is that it wholly concentrates on the so-called Feng-Shui concept. Feng-Shui is the ancient Chinese science of living in harmony with nature and one's surroundings – the art of balancing out the natural flow of energy in your surroundings so that you feel well, relaxed and thus able to improve your quality of life. All halls and rooms in the hotel are outfitted and decorated according to the principles of Feng-Shui creating an abundance of good vibrations.

Accommodation & Amenities

The hotel has 126 Superior rooms, 47 Deluxe rooms (both 48 square meters), 23 Junior Suites (68 square meters), two Senior Suites (88 square meters) as well as a President's Villa with 338 square meters.

The three restaurants, Good Chi, Le Bastide and Aigre-Doux provide everything that delights the gourmet's heart, ranging from richly-varied buffets to romantic dinners for two. Lovers can round off the day with a tropical cocktail in the picturesque surroundings in one of the three bars.

The bay is ideally suited to many forms of aquatic sports. You may use the hotel's own diving-centre and other facilities. Skilled instructors give beginners diving-lessons for a fee. There are a number of floodlit tennis courts and a bicycle rental service. You can also explore the fairytale island on mountain-bikes.

Honeymoon specials

Brides receive a 40 per cent discount throughout the year (except for the Christmas season from December 21 to January 7). This offer is valid only for Superior and Deluxe suites. Each bridal couple is given a basket of tropical fruit and sparkling wine. They are also served a romantic gala dinner.

The offer for couples celebrating their silver wedding anniversary is unique: The bride is given a price discount of 30 per cent in the above period. Here too, a complimentary basket of fruit, sparkling wine and a dinner for two are inclusive.

Prices/addresses

Accommodation in a Junior Suite costs from £ 115 per person and night, in Superior rooms from £ 75 per person and night.

Legends, Naiade Resorts
Pierre Simonet Street, Floreal
Mauritius/Ile Maurice
Tel: +230-698 98 00
Fax: +230-697 73 73

Beau Rivage*****

Multicultural elegance
Belle Mare, East Coast

This elegant hotel, located directly on a white sandy beach near Belle Mare, on the east coast of the island, reflects the varied culture of the dream-island of Mauritius. Chinese, Indian and African elements are merged with each other to create an extraordinary atmosphere. This is reflected by the use of straw-roofed buildings which are furnished with Indian and African woods and decorated with African textiles. The Restaurant Indochine provides an excellent multiethnic cuisine.

Accommodation & Amenities

The Maharajah Suite, with an area of 300 square meters, is the hotel's largest. Smaller suites are the 100 square meter Senior suites (extras: DVD-player, Jacuzzi) or the 90 square meter Junior suites (extras: Video-recorder, Jacuzzi). The Deluxe and Superior Rooms are about 60 square meters in area.

All rooms have a balcony or a terrace with sea-view, and an Internet connection in addition to the usual high standards of services provided.

Activities

The turquoise-coloured lagoon is most suitable for watersports and relaxing swims. For a charge, parasailing, deep-sea fishing, diving or an underwater stroll provide

variety. You can hire a bicycle, go horse-riding, or indulge yourself with a soothing massage. Costs for this are available on application. Sailing, water-skiing, canoeing, volleyball, tennis, aerobics and football are also on the programme.

Honeymoon specials

Brides receive a 50 per cent discount on the Superior and Deluxe suites from January 8 to October 31. A basket of tropical fruit, sparkling wine and a romantic dinner for two are included.

Prices/addresses

Depending on the season, a night in a double-room of the Superior category costs from about £ 105 per person.

Beau Rivage
Belle Mare
Ile Maurice
Tel: +230-402 20 00
Fax: +230-415 20 20

Les Pavillons****

Between mountain and sea
Le Morne Plage, south-west coast

The comfortable hotel Les Pavillons lies tucked away between a white sandy beach and the impressive mountain Le Morne Brabant in a bay with offshore coral-reefs. The crystal-clear water delights not only enthusiastic divers but also occasional swimmers and sunbathers and the beach is perfect for romantic walks.

Accommodation & Amenities
You can choose between exclusive Junior suites (52 square meters), Deluxe rooms (48 square meters), Superior rooms (46 square meters) and Standard rooms (42 square meters), all with a terrace or balcony facing the sea.

The hotel has a vast entrance area with lobby and reception-desk, the restaurant Le Benitier, an exclusive hairdresser's and a number of boutiques. Guests can enjoy the sea-view from the hotel's own swimming pool. Entertainment includes a sophisticated programme with live music each evening and once a week a Mauritian and a Creole show give an insight into the country's culture.

Activities
There is no better place for every form of aquatic sports than this wonderfully beautiful lagoon. It is the lovers' choice in Les Pavillons: surfing together, paddling-and canoeing outings, snorkelling or water-skiing. Volleyball or table-tennis, physical training or a match on one of the modern tennis-courts provide variety and you can relax in the sauna afterwards.

Massages and romantic sunset- and catamaran trips are available for a fee. Diving and fishing are also possible and, if you prefer firm ground under your feet, you can explore the neighbourhood by bike.

Honeymoon extras
The bride is given a 40 per cent discount for the Superior- and Deluxe suites (except in the Christmas season from December 21 to January 7). As a further extra, the bridal couple are given a basket of tropical fruit and a bottle of sparkling wine in their room and are served a romantic gala dinner. Not only newlyweds can let themselves be spoilt in Les Pavillons at special rates. All couples celebrating their silver wedding anniversary are granted discounts too; the "bride" pays 30 per cent less. Tropical fruits and sparkling wine in the room and a romantic dinner for two are also inclusive.

Prices/addresses
A night in a standard room costs from £ 60 per person.

Les Pavillons
La Pelouse, Le Morne
Ile Maurice
Tel: +230-401 40 00
Fax:+230-450 53 48

Belle Mare Plage*****

A new luxury-residence on a beautiful snow-white beach Belle Mare, East Coast

This luxury-hotel, a member of the Constance Hotels Group, was reopened in November 2002 on the lovely, two-kilometre-long Belle Mare sandy beach on the Mauritian east coast. Of the original Hotel only the renovated wing with the prestige rooms remains.

The hotel now offers excellent services to meet the most exacting demands. It is set in a tropical garden of almost 15 hectares where a breathtaking variety of colours and exotic scents welcome the bridal pair. The beach is protected by an offshore coral reef making it an ideal spot for water-sports or swimming. Port Louis, the capital, is about 45 minutes away, transfers to and from the airport take about an hour.

Accommodation & Amenities

The hotel-resort has 92 Prestige rooms (45 square meters, facing the sea), 137 Junior Suites (68 square meters, facing the sea, with a spacious terrace or balcony and a walk-in dressing-room) and six Deluxe Suites (96 square meters similarly-equipped to the Junior Suites with separate living-room and an extra shower and toilet). In addi-

tion, 17 villas with an area of 375 square meters (two bedrooms) and three villas with 525 square meters (three bedrooms and a separate dining-room) are available to the most highly selective clientele.

The tasteful, Mauritian Colonial-style furnishings are made in natural materials such as teak and marble. Each villa has a small, private enclosed garden area, a 28 square meters heated swimming-pool, a sundeck with sunbeds, and a pavilion. You have direct access to the ter-

race-garden from the living-room and bedroom on the ground floor. The outside bath adjoining the bathroom on the ground floor has a bathtub sunken in stone. A butler service is provided for guests with special wishes.

Four restaurants and five bars take you on a culinary journey. You have a splendid view of the beach and the vast pool from the restaurant La Citronelle. Buffet-style dinners with daily-changing themes are laid out there in a relaxed atmosphere each evening.
The La Spiaggia is set towards the beach and serves light meals and snacks throughout the day. Generous a la carte dinners are served there in the evening.
The Deer Hunter, set beside the golf-course, is a good venue, whether for a spot of exquisite refreshment during the day or an exclusive dinner in a cosy atmosphere.
The Blue Penny Café, the smallest of the restaurants, boasts not only first-class cuisine but also a wine- and cigar-lounge.

Activities
Water-sport enthusiasts truly get their money's worth in Belle Mare Plage. There is no extra charge for windsurfing, kayak, sailing, snorkelling, water-skiing, glass-bottom boat trips and pedalos. Use of the swimming pools, a fitness centre, four floodlit tennis courts, an air-conditioned squash court, table tennis, volleyball, minigolf and two 18-hole Championship Golf courses are free of charge. There is a fee only at the Links Golf Course for the compulsory club car.
Optimum provision is made for wellness fans: A Shiseido beauty institute gives you a wide range of massages and

body treatments for a fee. You may use the sauna with cold plunge-pool and turkish steam sauna in the wellness area at no cost.

Honeymoon extras
Belle Mare Plage welcomes guests to their room with a bottle of French champagne, flowers and canapes. They also treat them to a romantic candlelight dinner, creating an unforgettable atmosphere.

There is a 50 per cent bridal discount from May 1 to October 31. The bride is given a reduction of 25 per cent outside this period. The full price is valid merely from December 23 to January 6.

Prices/addresses
A night in Belle Mare Plage costs from about £ 70 per person, depending on the season.
Reservations with:

Infinity Specialist Tours Ltd.
Tel: 01491-57 14 54
Fax: 01491-63 61 59
e-mail: info@infinitytours.co.uk

The Residence Mauritius*****

An outing into the colonial era
Belle Mare, East Coast

"Escape from Normalcy", is the slogan of the Hotel Residence, one of the finest resorts on the east coast of Mauritius. This is the spot where the splendour and radiance of the past century come alive enrapturing visitors. Here they experience generous architecture, stately rooms and suites, an exquisite cuisine, an expansive pool-landscape and splendid gardens which reflect the Colonial lifestyle. The view from the hotel extends across one of the island's most beautiful white beaches with powdery sand to the Indian Ocean's kaleidoscope of colours.
The atmosphere is reminiscent of the 1920s and it is easy to forget the stress of everyday routine amidst the mixture of traditional and modern style.

Accommodation & Amenities
The hotel has 171 elegant rooms and suites with private terrace or balcony. The inner rooms, ranging from the "Garden View Room" (54 square meter) over "Ocean View" and "Ocean Front" to the two Royal Suites (220 square meter) are of natural materials and elegantly designed. Mostly natural stone, rattan and tropical wood were used.

The cuisine is inspired by Mauritius' multicultural influences. Apart from classical grilled dishes with an emphasis on fish, guests are also served meals with Chinese, Creole and Indian influences. Honeymooners can let themselves be spoilt from morning to evening in the bar, a 500 square meter lounge with upholstered suites and a large circular counter.

Activities
Beauty and wellness are the focal point of a stay in the Residence. Facial treatments, shiatsu- and foot reflexzone massages, pedicures, manicures, acupressure, lymph drainage, steam baths and body peeling are available for a fee. A beautician designs an individual beauty-plan for the guest from the comprehensive programme. Nine rooms are available for treatments. The one in the middle of the tropical garden is the highlight: The relaxation programme works twice as well with the view of the lagoon and a mild ocean-breeze.

Diving, deep-sea fishing, and catamaran outings or horse riding is available for a fee. Water-skiing, windsurfing, snorkelling, canoeing and kayaking, the three tennis courts, volleyball, aerobics and physical training are complimentary. The sauna and steam bath may also be used for free.

Honeymoon extras
The Residence grants a 100 per cent bridal discount in the categories Ocean View and Ocean Front for a minimum stay of seven nights with breakfast. This is the only Hotel on the Island to do so. However the offer is not valid for the period from December 21 to January 5.

The hotel also has arrangements for couples celebrating their wedding anniversary. They can choose from four packages for a minimum stay of seven nights within one month before or after the anniversary:

Package 1
Exotic bowl of fruit, a bottle of champagne, one beauty treatment per person, a beach-bag, straw-hats, a refreshing spray, a pareo, a T-shirt.

Package 2
Exotic bowl of fruit, a bottle of champagne, a private candlelight dinner, inclusive of a bottle of wine

Package 3
Exotic bowl of fruit, a bottle of champagne, an island-tour: Pampelmousses Botanic Gardens, Port Louis and Domaine Les Pailles.

Package 4
Exotic bowl of fruit, a bottle of champagne, a catamaran excursion including lunch and drinks.

Prices/addresses
Accommodation in a standard room costs from about £ 130 per person and night.

The Residence Mauritius
Coastal Road
Belle Mare, Mauritius
Tel: +230-401 88 88
Fax: +230-415 58 88

Air Mauritius

Mauritius, the Pearl of the Indian Ocean, is the place for an unforgettable holiday 365 days a year. Your holiday starts on board the plane as soon as you embarque and the small tropical bird "paille en queue" is not the Air Mauritius symbol without good reason. Passengers are just as impressed with the five-star service as with the bird's elegant, smooth flight which delights watchers time and again.

The airline's history is still relatively young. It was established in 1967 to promote tourism as the second economic base for the island that is still fully dependent on sugar cultivation. Air Mauritius advanced in recent years to become a byword for luxury worldwide, thanks to its courteous service and high standards.

Today, Air Mauritius is one of the world's strongest-growing airlines on account of its solid corporate policy. It has one of the most modern fleets at its disposal, with 14 aircraft currently, and flies to 28 destinations on all continents, including ten in Europe. Owing to the extensive network of routes, a variety of combinations in the Indian Ocean are possible. Holidaymakers from the UK are able to fly from Heathrow four times a week. The Airbus A340 is deployed on this route.

Passengers on the Airbus A340 can choose between Economy-, Business- and First Class. Air Mauritius takes the best interests of the economy passengers seriously. With 84 centimetres legroom in both plane-models, the airline is one with the most space between Economy Class seats. The finest food and drinks as well as the proverbial Mauritian hospitality on board literally make time fly.

Passengers are also able to use a helicopter on Mauritius, whether for breathtaking trips around the island or for timesaving transfers from the airport to the hotel. They also enjoy further advantages on the ground or when making reservations. You may take along 15 kilograms of extra sports gear free of charge if you register this in advance. Similarly, reserving your seat when booking guarantees the place you wish.

Honeymoon extras
Couples are given a small sweet surprise on board to get them into the right mood for the imminent honeymoon.

Prices/address
Package tours with Air Mauritius to Mauritius and its neighbouring islands from:

Infinity Specialist Tours Ltd.
71a Bell Street
Henley-on-Thames
Oxon. RG9 2BD
England
Tel: 01491-57 15 45
Fax: 01491-63 61 59
e-mail: info@infinitytours.co.uk

Indonesia/Bali

countless sculptures of various deities that merge with the agricultural landscape into a charming holiday scene.

Bali has a consistently warm tropical climate because of its close proximity to the equator. The average temperature is 29° C, water temperature about 28° C. A constant breeze ensures a pleasant climate in the coastal region despite the humidity.

The dry season is from April to October, while the rainy season lasts from November to March when most showers are heavy but brief. Thai Airways, Cathay Pacific, Lauda Air and Qantas fly to Bali several times a week.

Bali lies in the middle of the Indonesian archipelago between Java Sea in the North and the Indian Ocean in the south. The archipelago between Asia and Australia is the world's largest island state encompassing 13,677 islands. Nearly three million Balinese live on the island of 5,620 kilometres, most of them in the capital Denpasar.

The majority inhabit small unspoilt villages scattered throughout the island between uncountable rice-paddies. A volcanic mountain range, the highest peak of which is called Gunung Agung – Centre of the Universe – stretches from east to west.

Unlike the Islamic-characterised island of Java, just two kilometres away, most Balinese are followers of the Hindu faith. This is reflected in the ornate temple-sites and

"House arrest" and a meal of rice
The big wedding celebration with friends and distant relatives of the couple takes place in Bali a few days before the religious ceremony. The pair, lavishly decorated with gold, celebrates exuberantly with the guests, who bear mainly items of food such as rice, coffee or sugar as gifts. After this festivity which, like the entire wedding, is arranged by the groom's family, the couple begin a three-day "trial period" during which they may not leave the house and are excluded from village life. The wedding ceremony, in which a priest calls on the gods and requests their blessings for the couple, takes place in the family-temple only after this phase. The highlight of the ritual is the couple's feeding each other with rice, symbolising their willingness to take care of each other in future.

Matahari Beach Resort & Spa*****

A holiday for body and soul
Singaraja

The Matahari Beach Resort & Spa receives its guests in the north-western part of Bali on a fine, black sandy lava beach near Pemuteran and in close vicinity to the Bali Barat National Park, an area still largely unspoilt by tourism. The hotel was built in traditional Balinese style. Balinese craftsmen and artists used only local materials such as marble, paras, palemanan, wood and bamboo, to create a resort that is perfectly integrated into the countryside.

The Matahari Beach Resort & Spa propagates integrated tourism. Just as local customs and practices exercised their natural influence in the building of the resort, so do visitors have the opportunity to become acquainted with the complexity of Balinese culture. This takes the form of lessons in wood-carving and cookery or gamelan dance as well as of physical fitness, thanks to a refined wellness programme.

Accommodation & Amenities

Guests are accommodated in the resort's 16 bungalows. There is a choice of four different categories according to taste – Garden View, Premium Garden View, Deluxe and Super Deluxe.

The bungalows differ in location, size and equipment. What they all have in common, however is a two-winged, hand-carved Balinese door leading into the bed-living room. This room is decorated in subdued warm colours and the furniture includes a king-size Balinese bed or two separate beds. The lighting which gives the wood a warm glow is a particularly ingenious feature.

Each bungalow has individually adjustable remote controlled air-conditioning, telephone, mini-bar and an electronic safe. Each unit includes a marble bathroom with a king-size tub, a private back garden with tropical plants and an open-air shower shaped like a water-spouting Balinese dragon.

The Deluxe- and Super Deluxe Bungalows are equipped additionally with double washbasins and bidets. The Super Deluxe Bungalow has another extra available: a private pavilion in the middle of a lotus pond.

In the Devi Ramona Restaurant, like everywhere else in Matahari Beach Resort and Spa, Eastern and Western influences provide exciting contrasts that are a special delight for the palate. You can discover the secrets of this exotic cuisine in professionally-conducted cookery classes if you wish.

A private wine-cellar, a unique architectural specimen on Bali and worthy of a visit in any event, supplements the gourmet cuisine perfectly and offers a wide selection of high-quality wines. The Wayang Cocktail Bar is the resort's main rendezvous. Guests meet here before and after dinner to enjoy a wide choice of classic drinks and fruit-based cocktails.

The Parwathi Spa is another highlight in Matahari Beach Resort & Spa. Its design is in the style of the Balinese royal water-palaces and is based on the interplay between water and earth as the source of relaxation and inspiration.

Today one enjoys a very special form of wellness here, known as "The Touch of Bali". The treatments are based on traditional massaging techniques carried out with essential oils and essences by two specialists working in perfect synchronisation.

Activities
Matahari Beach Resort & Spa has an extensive range of sports on offer, in particular water sports. The freshwater pool, measuring 23 x 11 metres, and the lava beach with crystal-clear seawater and only minor tidal changes provide ideal conditions for snorkelling and diving. Motor- and glass-bottomed boats tempt people to take short or long outings. You are also able to play tennis, badminton or golf and to explore the scenic beauty of the island on mountainbike- or trekking-tours.

Prices/addresses
A night in Matahari Beach Resort & Spa costs from about £ 80 per person, including breakfast, and from about £ 180 in a suite.

Matahari Beach Resort
P.O. Box 194, Pemuteran
Singaraja, Bali, Indonesia
Tel: +62-36 29 23 12
Fax: +62-362 92 313

Wedding Package
"Balinese Fairytale"

Matahari Beach Resort fulfils dreams and organizes weddings for lovers' on the "islands of gods". The couples receive a special welcome are accommodated in a luxurious villa with a private back-garden and enjoy all of the resort's amenities.

The wedding day starts off at an entirely relaxed pace with a Balinese massage in the beach-pavilion. Willing hands help to dress those who choose the traditional wedding costume.

A representative of the local tourist agency waits for the couple with all of the necessary marriage documents. A boat takes the newlyweds on a mini-cruise after the ceremony that is accompanied by festive speeches and typical Gamelan music. An intimate candlelight dinner, served on the beach, is the closing highlight of this memorable day.

What deadlines are to be observed?
A wedding on Bali can take place immediately after arrival, provided that the required documents have reached the tour-operator at least eight weeks before the date.

What documents are necessary?
Important note: a civil wedding on Bali is only possible in combination with a religious marriage!
▶ A passport valid for at least six months after landing, plus copies of the first six pages
▶ Birth certificates or certified copies thereof
▶ Certificate of No Impediment to Marrtiage
▶ Six black-and-white passport pictures 6x4 cm, bride and groom together (the man on the right, the woman on the left)
▶ Catholic couples: "Transfer for Marriage Abroad" form (issued by the home diocese), accompanied by a baptismal certificate
▶ Protestants: Declaration of Consent from the home diocese (informal), accompanied by a baptismal certificate
▶ Documents for marrying couples of different denominations are available on request.

Services included:
▶ Airport-hotel-airport transfer in an air-conditioned limousine
▶ Seven nights with buffet-style breakfast in a premium Garden View Bungalow
▶ Welcoming cocktail, floral arrangement
▶ Traditional Balinese massage
▶ Religious and civil ceremony on the beach with an officiating clergyman and a registry-official
▶ Musical accompaniment by two Gamelan musicians at the beach-wedding
▶ Bouquet of orchids
▶ Photographer, 36 pictures and negatives
▶ Short sunset-cruise, including cocktails
▶ Romantic five-course dinner on the beach with a private waiter, wine and music
▶ Room-service breakfast with sparkling-wine the next morning
▶ Outing to Munsuk waterfall and to Tambligan Lake
▶ Assistance with registering, arranging and certifying the marriage, sworn German translation of the marriage certificate
▶ all local fees

Price per couple: About £ 1,240

PACIFIC
OCEAN

French-Polynesia

The islands of French Polynesia are lined up in a vivid green chain in the middle of the blue Pacific. Tahiti, also called the "Island of Love", is the largest of the 118 islands. Its landmarks are tropical rainforests, cascading waterfalls and the two volcanoes more than 2,000 metres high. The news of the island's legendary beauty, immortalised on canvas by the impressionist Paul Gauguin, made the island group the epitome of the romantic South Sea paradise in the early 20th century.

A trace of South Sea romance, combined with the French flair of the Colonial era, still surrounds Tahiti today. Papeete, the capital of the island-state, has all of the necessary facilities of a modern city available, such as a hospital, banks, entertainment facilities and a significant port.

You need not fear that your holiday literally becomes a wash-out as there are many sunny days, even in the rainy season (November to April). Rain is not to be expected from May to October; the climate is mild and dry then. However, it never becomes too hot, temperatures are between 25° and 30° C throughout the year. The flight with Air New Zealand or Air France to the South Sea paradise takes about 20 hours.

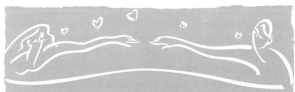

Separate wedding celebrations

In Polynesia's pre-Christian society, the wedding ceremony took place only in the presence of the bridal couple and the bride's family. All of those present sat on a large mat, the couple at one end and the bride's family at the other.
During the ceremony, each guest brought the couple a package of sugarcane, which a priest then offered as a burnt sacrifice. After the ritual, the bridegroom tore up the mat and gave the strips of cloth to children. The wedding-party then moved on to the house of the bridegroom's parents, where two celebrations were held - one for the women and another for the men.

Tahiti Honeymoon Voucher

Polynesian wedding on Moorea

Bridal couples who wish to make the most beautiful moment an unforgettable experience can exchange vows symbolically once again after the civil wedding-ceremony in UK. Dreams of a wedding in traditional Polynesian style come true in the folklore- and cultural centre Tiki Village on Moorea. The couples are welcomed with music and dancing on arrival in the village and then prepared for the wedding separately.

While the bride is being massaged with coconut-milk and dressed like a Tahitian princess, the groom is dressed as a chieftain and, like his fiancee, is given a crown of flowers and a garland of blossoms (lei). The priest extends an invitation into the stone-temple for the marriage-ceremony.

During the ceremony, the women of Tiki Village sing religious songs; a dance in honour of the newlyweds is presented afterwards. Finally, the bridal couple is driven into the sunset on board a royal canoe to the accompaniment of ukulele- and guitar-music. A candlelight dinner in Tiki Village or in a Beachcomber hotel brings the proceedings to a close.

Honeymoon by voucher

Various hotels on the islands of Tahiti, Moorea, Bora Bora and Huahine offer wedding-travellers honeymoon specials such as discounts on the regular room-prices. In addition, the Tahiti Honeymoon Vouchers created for the destination French Polynesia provide bridal couples with the possibility of allowing their guests to present them with a piece of luck, namely, their dream honeymoon on Tahiti and its islands. The vouchers can be obtained by wedding guests from Infinity Specialist Tours. They are offered to the value of £ 25, £ 50 and £ 100.

This is how it works: The couple plan their individual dream trip with the tour operator. Afterwards, they inform their guests about their desired gifts by means of a specially-printed information leaflet. The wedding-guests are then able to order the Tahiti Wedding Vouchers from Infinity and hand it to the couple in a special envelope at the wedding. The couple then exchange the voucher for the honeymoon trip to Tahiti and its islands at the responsible travel organisers.

Further information on the Tahiti Honeymoon Vouchers:
Infinity Specialist Tours Ltd.
Tel: 01491-57 15 45
Fax: 01491-63 61 59

General information on "Tahiti and its Islands" from:
Tahiti Tourisme
Tel: 020-7771-70 23
Fax: 020-7771-70 59
e-mail: tahiti@cibgroup.co.uk

(Design may be differing)

Moorea Beachcomber
Intercontinental Resort*****

Paradise for nature-lovers and wellness-fans
Papetoai

Moorea lies northwest of Tahiti and is the location of the Moorea Beachcomber Intercontinental Resort, a paradise for romantics, nature-lovers and all who want to let themselves be truly spoilt for once. Exotic fauna and flora in the water and on land are only waiting to be discovered. For instance, by yacht, on an outing with the glass-bottomed boat or on horseback along the white beaches.

Accommodation & Amenities
Accommodation is available in Overwater Bungalows, Garden Bungalows and spacious guestrooms, all equipped with ceiling-fans or air-conditioning, mini-bar, telephone and TV. Dinner in the restaurant Fare Nui is a culinary experience. Delicious food is also served in the poolside-restaurant Fare Hana. Enjoy exquisite cocktails and picturesque sunsets in the popular Motu Iti bar! Seafood buffets and Tahitian shows in the evening are among the resort's highlights. A fitness- and wellness-area, volleyball, tennis, diving, swimming with dolphins, waterskiiing are windsurfing are some of the other activities.

Wellness
French-born Helene Sillinger opened a spa in the Beachcomber Intercontinental in 1996. The former assistant to a plastic surgeon, nutrition- and fitness expert, masseur and nature-therapist uses only cosmetics made from fresh fruits, spices and blossoms. Couples can also enjoy the relaxing programme together, for example, a bath and massage with coconut-milk.

Prices/addresses
A night at honeymoon-tariff in an Overwater Bungalow costs from about £ 125 per person.

Moorea Beachcomber International Resort
Papetoai, Moorea
French Polynesia
Tel: +689-55 19 19
Fax: +689-55 19 55
www.tahitiresorts.com

Reservations at Infinity Specialist Tours Ltd.
Tel: 01491-57 15 45
Fax: 01491-63 61 59

Fiji

The first word of welcome for visitors to Fiji is "Bula". "Bula – Hello, how are you?" is a magical word on the Fiji islands and reflects the open and hospitable nature of the islanders. Visitors can also bring a smile to the lips of every Fijian by calling out a cheerful "Bula" in return.

The difference between Fiji and other South Sea Islands is the untouched jungle vegetation covering 65 per cent of the island's surface.

Many activities, such as mountain hikes, boat trips, horseback riding, rafting and much more, are available to visitors who, besides the beaches, sun and sea, also want to visit the interior.

The Fiji islands have a mild tropical climate. Southeast tradewinds ensure dry weather from May to October. The rainy season lasts from December to April, with much less rainfall on the islands to the west than those to the east.

The quickest connection from UK takes about 22 hours. Air New Zealand flies visitors directly from London Heathrow to Nadi with a stopover in Los Angeles. Nadi is located on Viti Levu, Fiji's main island.

A Fijian Honeymoon

Strict rules intended to strengthen the political alliances between the respective clans, among other things, were applied to marriage on the Fiji islands in the past. Nowadays, Fijians are relatively free to select their partner and the traditional ceremony was replaced by a church wedding. Previously, a new house was built for the couple in the bridegroom's village after he paid a price to the bride's parents. This house was laid out with numerous mats of tapa - material made from bark - by the groom's female relatives. On the wedding-day, the couple and their relations gathered there. The groom's family took care of the festive meal from which the couple first ate alone after a brief ceremony. The guests consumed the rest as soon as the bride and groom were finished. The mats were collected in the evening and a nuptial bed prepared for the young couple. The newlyweds were then left to honeymoon in the privacy of their new home for four days, during which their families provided them with food.

Maravu Plantation Resort****

The Island of Flowers
Taveuni

The Maravu Plantation Resort stands on the garden-island Taveuni, the third largest of the nearly 320 Fiji Islands. Taveuni fascinates people with its unique fauna, secluded lakes and waterfalls, black- and white sandy beaches, high mountains and, not least of all, the warmth of its native population.

The island has long been one of the Top Ten for divers due to its unique undersea world. The 26-hour flight with Air New Zealand is worthwhile, especially during a European winter. It is springtime in these latitudes then and Taveuni is submerged in a sea of blossoms.

The Maravu Plantation Resort reflects Taveuni's image in miniature. Its 100-metres-long sandy beach is skirted by rainforest trees and palms. The complex is a former coconut plantation that was transformed into a blooming tropical garden in recent years.

It is ideal for honeymooners seeking tranquillity because the hotel has space for just 20 guests.

Accommodation & Amenities

Fourteen "bures", houses in the national language, are tucked away in the spacious tropical garden. They are all built in such a way as to give a clear view of the tropical sunset.

All of them are tastefully decorated with precious woods and textiles, bamboo walls, rattan furniture and ceramic objects. A ventilator, a comfortable bath/toilet and a mini-bar are among the standard amenities in the five deluxe houses, the three honeymoon houses and both halves of the semi-detached houses.

Lodgers in the honeymoon "bures" – like all the "bures", these are absolutely private – have the unusual luxury of an open-air shower and their own sundeck.

The main building overlooks the pool and includes the lobby, restaurant, lounge and a small library of literature on the country and its people. The restaurant is open on all sides and spoils guests with Indian, Creole or Fijian cuisine.

Once a week, a fete is held at which you can enjoy not only traditional dances but also try a typical meal prepared in a clay-oven. A tip: you can leave your watch at home as hotel guests are summoned to meals by lali drums.

Activities

The resort has a swimming-pool, tennis court, children's playground, kayaks and horses available. The German landlord, Jochen Kiess, and his team ensure that tourists get to know the scenic attractions of the island on jungle treks and Landcruiser excursions.

The resort's private ten-metre yacht takes them to snorkel and dive at Rainbow Reef and the famous Great White Wall, two of the world's leading underwater paradises. Deep-sea fishermen may indulge in their passion on board the hotel-yacht.

Prices/addresses

A night in the "bure" costs from about £ 75 per person with half-board (obligatory); children under 14 are free.

Maravu Plantation
Postal Agency Matei Taveuni
Fiji
Tel: +679-888-05 85
Fax: +679-888-06 00
e-mail: maravu@connect.com.fj

Contact address in Europe:
Jochen and Angela Kiess
Lehmgrubenstr. 44
D-70188 Stuttgart
Tel: +49-711-262 37 53
Fax: +49-711-262 47 09

Hawaii

Big Island, commonly known as Hawaii, is the largest of the six Hawaiian islands. Big Island's landscape is very varied, depending on topography and climate. Snow falls regularly in the mountains during winter, the relatively rainy eastern coast is known for its wealth of orchids. An impressive desert area stretches out in the south and the valleys of the north are fertile farmlands overlooked by five volcanoes of which Mauna Loa and Kilauea are still active.

Numerous temples, religious festivals and the famous hula dance festivals are cultural highlights. Although not the ideal destination for a purely seaside holiday, due to the black lava beaches, a refreshing swim is always possible, especially along the wind-protected west coast, where it seldom rains. The climate is moderate and temperatures remain between 24° and 27° C throughout the year.

Oahu Island boasts the world famous Waikiki beach and is 50 minutes flying time Northwest of the Big Island. Its city airport of Honolulu is linked with Los Angeles and San Francisco by a number of international airlines including United and Delta. Flights from Europe take about 19 hours, there are inter-island airlines flying daily regular services to the Neighbouring Islands including Maui and Hawaii.

Like Big Island, Oahu is an island of contrasts. In the south there are Honolulu's crowded city-centres and Waikiki's hotel-skyscrapers, in the north rocky coasts and beaches with banana- and sugarcane plantations in the background, or natural rainforests in the mountain-regions.

The white, sandy beaches, the secluded inlets and the imposing cliffs that divide the sections of the beaches make the island a very desirable honeymoon destination. Visitors seeking to escape the bustle of Waikiki will find numerous spots away from the population centre,

for example, at Lanakei Beach on the north coast. The very rugged Koolau Mountain Range that functions as a climatic divider extends across the island from northwest to southeast. Thus, there is considerably more rain in northern and northeastern Oahu than in the south. On the whole, the climate is mild and equable with year-round temperatures between 24° and 27° C.

Of all Hawaiian islands, Maui is said to offer the richest diversity. It became famous mainly because of the legendary sunset above the Haleakala crater, which captivates even the less romantic, and because of the Pacific that surges here towards the coast and made the island a surfers' Mecca. Numerous opportunities on land, rugged mountains from which roaring waterfalls tumble into the valleys and Lahaina, the former capital of the Hawaiian kingdom, are an alternative if water sports are not your thing.

White Dream Wedding Honolulu

Hawaii is still a synonym for the South Sea dream. The group of islands however has developed into a modern metropolis with big-city bustle against a palm-beach setting. Numerous, completely different venues are available for weddings as a result. These range from the ocean-view chapel to the botanical private park and the fairytale beach.

What documents are necessary?
▸ Passport that is valid for the duration of the stay
▸ Wedding permit which is issued locally after arrival
▸ If widowed or divorced: Proof by death- or divorce-certificate
▸ For minors: Sworn translation of a declaration of permission from the legal guardians (minimum age for marriage is 16 years)

Services included
▸ Three nights in the luxury-hotel Sheraton Moana Surfrider
▸ Wedding-ceremony in the Calvary-by-the-Sea Church with a view of the ocean and reef, or in the tropical private park Pua Melia, or on Lani Kai beach
▸ Marriage by an independent member of the clergy witnesses, organiser
▸ Flower-garlands (leis) for bride and groom
▸ Bridal bouquet
▸ Transfer in a luxury limousine
▸ Champagne during the return-trip
▸ Photographer, including 24 pictures and negatives
▸ Organist or solo musician
▸ Souvenir marriage-certificate, 20 personal wedding-cards to be sent out to relations and friends
▸ Assistance with registration for the Hawaii Marriage License and certification
▸ All local fees

Price per couple from about £ 1,990

The Fairmont
Kea Lani Hotel*****

White Dream Holidays
Wailea

Hawaii's only holiday-complex with luxury suites, Kea Lani Hotel Suites & Villas, in 1991 at Maui's southern tip on the famous Polo Beach. "Kea Lani" can be roughly translated as "heavenly-white" and the sparkling-white facade is really a striking contrast to the greenery of the more than 2,000-hectare tropical garden and the forever-blue sky. The complex, designed by architect Jose Luis Esquerra, brings a touch of Mediterranean flair to Maui and combines the romance of an island with the luxury of a suite-hotel.

Accommodation & Amenities
An extra-wide veranda with ocean-view characterises the 413 spacious, luxuriously-furnished suites on the five floors of the main building. Apart from separate living-and bedrooms, all suites have colour TV, video-recorder, laser disc- and CD-player, radio and telephone. Further comforts include built-in safes, additional TV sets in the bedrooms, dual telephone lines, a bar-niche, refrigerator, microwave oven and coffee-maker. The marble-tiled bathroom with bathtub, separate shower-cubicle, twin washbasins, hairdryer, bathrobes and exclusive toiletries, also satisfies every wish. Each of the nearly 80 square metres suites has individually-adjustable air-conditioning and ceiling-fans. The two- to four-room villas of between 90 and 200 square metres are set even closer to the sea.

The restaurants Kea Lani, Caffe Ciao and Polo Beach Grille & Bar serve creations from the Euro-Pacific cuisine at tastefully-decorated tables. All ingredients are market-fresh, vegetables and herbs come from Maui's highland gardens. A wide selection of wines and tropical beverages is also available.

Activities
You have a choice of five first-class golf -courses, including those in Wailea, Waikapu and Makena. Tennis buffs are able to have a romp on the 14 courts of the nearby tennis-club. The range of activities also includes windsurfing, kayaking, snorkelling, scuba diving and courses in almost every form of water-sport. The Kea Lani Spa takes care of relaxation and well-being. The elegant recuperation centre provides a variety of soothing treatments and products from all over the world and the modern fitness-centre is open around the clock.

Honeymoon extras/wedding
The Royal Fountain Terrace is a very special spot for bridal couples. This highlight of the garden complex with softly-splashing waterfalls is a popular venue for wedding receptions.

Prices/addresses
A night in the Ocean View Suite cost from about £ 224 per person.

Kea Lani Hotel
4100 Wailea Alanui, Wailea
Maui, Hawaii 96753, USA
Tel: 001-808-875 41 00
Fax: 001-808-875 12 00

Weddings on Maui are also organized locally, see page 91, Tel: +1-808-249 64 90, Fax: +1-808-875 74 14.

Romantic Maui Wedding

A Wedding Co-ordination Office was established on Maui in 1996 under the management of wedding-expert Claudia Schnetz (bookings through Infinity, Tel: 01491-57 15 45).

She arranges weddings with a personal touch, from the simple beach-wedding to the luxurious wedding package, inclusive of a stretch-limousine, photographer, video, rental of a private park or at a waterfall that is accessible only by helicopter.

It goes without saying that the complete documentary service for recognition in the UK is included.

What documents are necessary?
▶ Passport valid for the length of the stay
▶ Marriage Permit (is issued locally)
▶ If widowed or divorced: Proof by death- or divorce certificate
▶ For minors (minimum age 16 years): declaration of permission from the legal guardians

Example of a comprehensive package:
▶ Wedding ceremony in a small historical church by the sea or in a tropical private garden with a magnificent view
▶ Transfer by limousine from the hotel and back

Maui Rites
Garlands of flowers and money
In traditional Hawaiian society, marriage rites were performed only in headmen's families. The bridal couple's hands were joined with garlands of flowers (leis) as a symbol of their togetherness.
Nowadays, Hawaiians get married according to their religion. The couples are always decorated with leis regardless of the rites. The bride and groom are congratulated during the "money dance". The guests decorate them with garlands of paper money and wish them luck while they are dancing.

▶ Champagne on the return journey
▶ Witnesses / co-ordinator
▶ Flower-garlands (leis) and bridal bouquet
▶ Solo guitarist
▶ Photographer, including 24 pictures and negatives
▶ Souvenir marriage-certificate and 20 personal wedding-cards to be sent out to relations and friends
▶ Sworn translation of the marriage certificate and international certification
▶ Assistance with registration and certification
▶ All local fees

Price per couple about £ 2,100

CARIBBEAN

Antigua

If a honeymoon trip could last for a whole year, then newlyweds could swim at a different beach on Antigua each day. Reputedly, exactly 365 fine sandy beaches surround the tiny Caribbean island of 108 square miles.

Coral reefs extend along the front of the fantastic beaches, a genuine paradise for snorkellers and divers. No wonder, because with a visibility of up to 30 metres, even inexperienced underwater sportsmen can easily discover the secrets of the ocean depths with a wealth of flora and fauna.

The wreck of the Andes, a sailing-ship that sank more than a century ago in Deep Bay, close to the capital St. John's, also brings variety to the underwater outings. Surfers too, appreciate Antigua's coastline; the professionals launch their boards in the east of the island, the inexperienced on the protected west coast.

You can dive for wrecks on Antigua and track history on dry land. The best-known building on the island is Nelson's Dockyard in English Harbour, the world's only remaining Georgian port. Shirley Heights, one of the island's many hills, gives you an impressive view of the Old City and the port, enhanced by live steelband- and reggae music on Sundays.

The weather is optimal. The average daily temperature is about 28°C with only very slight rainfall. Somewhat heavier showers occur in from September to November. Condor flies every Friday from Germany to Antigua, British Airways several times weekly via London.

Jolly Beach Resort ***

A spacious all-inclusive domicile
St. John's

Jolly Beach Resort is located on one of Antigua's most beautiful beaches. The detached Moorish-style houses, built no higher than the tallest palms and nestled in a huge tropical garden-complex, stretch along the almost two-kilometres-long, white sandy beach. Guests have a wonderful view – as far as the neighbouring islands of St.Kitt-Nevis and Redonda – across the sea shimmering in a thousand shades of blue.

Accommodation & Amenities

The 462 rooms of the Jolly Beach Resort are furnished Moorish style and equipped with air-conditioning, radio, telephone and TV. Resident Manager Baerbel Pfeiffer knows the preferences of European visitors and includes them in her plans. You have a fantastic view of the sea and the tropical garden from all of the rooms. The resort also features a highly-varied culinary programme. No less than five restaurants provide a great selection of Italian, Caribbean-, international-, Greek-, fish- and seafood dishes. Guests will never be bored; even selecting a cold drink can be exiting. You can choose from seven bars in the complex, one of them in the middle of a vast fantasy-pool. The cyber-cafe, the beach-hucksters village, the port opposite the hotel and a golf course are other points of interest.

Activities

All-inclusive clientele have tennis-courts, a games-room with billiards and table-tennis, as well as a fitness-gym at their disposal. All forms of water-sports, "motorised" ones excepted, are free of charge. Jolly Beach's entertainment crew offers a variety programme during the day; bands, shows and a disco are on in the evening.

Honeymoon/weddings

A wedding co-ordinator in Jolly Beach takes cares of the entire wedding package. The bridal couples merely express their wishes and look forward to their big day.

The arrangement includes the fees for the wedding and all associated formalities, the bridal bouquet, wedding-cake, champagne, hors d'oeuvres and the festive decoration of the gazebo. You have a choice between two chapels or exchanging vows directly on the beach. The co-ordinator will also accomodate special wishes.

Prices/address

A night (all-inclusive) in a standard-room costs from about £ 89.

Postal address:
Jolly Beach Resort
P.O. Box W2009
St. John's Antigua, West Indies
Tel: 268-462-0061
Fax: 268-562-2302
www.jollybeach resort.com

British Virgin Islands

Peace and quiet, seclusion and privacy, time just for yourself and your partner. Is this your dream of a perfect honeymoon?

On the British Virgin Islands, you find no huge crowds, no casinos, skyscrapers or fast-food restaurants, not even a traffic-light. Instead, the islands fascinate you with secluded dream-beaches, luxury hotels, small guest-houses, hospitable locals and a landscape that is untouched to a large extent. Is it a wonder that they are described as "Nature's little secrets"?

The nearly 60 islands and islets, some of them uninhabited, lie far from the beaten tourist track in the northern Caribbean, about 100 kilometres east of Puerto Rico. Nevertheless, they can be reached comfortably from Europe within a day. They are close to each other and

thus are ideal for island-hopping. Tortola, Virgin Gorda, Jost Van Dyke and Anegeda are the largest and best-known.

The waters surrounding the islands have a reputation as one of the world's best territories for sailing, offering both beginners and professionals perfect conditions for long trips. This is due to the constant trade winds and the outstanding infrastructure.

All of the islands, except for Anegada, are of volcanic origin. You can take fantastic walks in the mountains and shop in small businesses. Naturally, the main attractions are the beach and the turquoise sea for sunbathing, swimming, snorkelling and diving.

You can also exchange your wedding vows on the virtually untouched islands. The sole condition is that you spend three days there before the wedding.

Further information about your honeymoon or wedding on the British Virgin Islands is available from the British Virgin Islands Tourist Board under:

Tel: +44-207-94 78 20
Fax: +44-207-947 82 79
e-mail: bvi@bho.fcb.com
www.bvitouristboard.com

Long Bay Beach Resort & Villas****

Pure luxury
Tortola, British Virgin Islands

Countless bays and secluded caves dot the coastline of the Virgin Islands, where the Caribbean Sea and the Atlantic Ocean meet. For centuries, they protected seafarers and hid smugglers. Today the islands attract tourists who enjoy exploring the countryside. Most of them visit Tortola, the main island of the British Virgin Islands.

The generously laid-out four-star hotel stands at Long Bay, about 20 kilometres from the airport and 14 kilometres from the capital Road Town.

The unique location in a large park with exotic trees, directly at the long, white sandy beach, promises restful holidays in quiet, elegant surroundings. One of the swimming-pools stands near to the beach; another very large

one with whirlpool and bar is on a slightly higher level on the Pelican Terrace. The complex has various restaurants and bars as well as the Beach Cafe for snacks in a former sugar mill. The excellent Garden Restaurant receives dinner-guests, while the Pool Bar and Terry's Bar pamper them with Caribbean cocktails.

Accommodation & Amenities
The resort has 115 rooms in various categories. The Hillside Oceanview rooms and suites are about 100 metres from the beach and the Junior Suites Hillside Oceanview Deluxe, with seating-units, about 70 metres from the beach. Some of them stand close to the swimming-pool. The Beachfront Deluxe rooms provide additional changing-rooms and separate showers, the romantic cabanas stand on stilts directly at the seaside. Luxurious two- or three-bedroom villas with a living-room, kitchen and a large terrace with grill are available with a private pool on request.
All rooms have air-conditioning, cable TV, direct-dialling telephone with modem, refrigerator, coffee-maker, hairdryer, safe and a balcony or ocean-view terrace.

Activities

The complex offers three tennis courts – two of them floodlit – snorkelling-gear, a nine-hole pitch-and-putt course, a well-equipped fitness centre and a small but fine spa with a wide range of treatments to pamper you and ensure your well-being. Here you are able not only to enjoy various massages but are also taught how to massage your partner.

Another attraction is Mahogany Run, an 18-hole golf course, located in St. Thomas, an hour's boatride away. An extra department of the hotel organises sailing- and diving-trips, excursions for fishermen and horsemen, as well as outings in the surrounding area.

Honeymoon extras/weddings

This hotel is ideal for weddings and honeymoons. Your celebration will be arranged entirely according to your wishes. Marriage Organiser Astrid Wenzke is in charge of arrangements. The wedding-package includes a priest, witnesses if desired, a bottle of champagne, a cake, wedding decorations and a roll of film that is developed before you leave.

You choose the venue whether on the beach with your toes in the sand or at one of the many other romantic places available at the resort. The hotel organises a romantic dinner or a big wedding reception for you at your request. Bridal couples pay the price for 12 days of a 14-day stay (from June 1 to December 20).

Prices/addresses

A night in a Hillside Oceanview room costs from about £ 49 per person.

Postal address:
Long Bay Beach Resort & Villas
P.O. Box 433, West End, Tortola
British Virgin Islands
Tel: 001-800-729 95 99
Fax: 001-284-495 42 52
www.longbay.com

Flight-connections:
British Airways to Antigua, ongoing flight with Liat. KLM or Air France to St. Maarten, ongoing flight with Liat.

Little Dix Bay*****

Garden- and beach paradise
Virgin Gorda, British Virgin Islands

The cordial staff of the Little Dix Bay welcome you at the international airport of Tortola-Beef Island. An ocean yacht takes you in just 30 minutes directly to the island of Virgin Gorda, one of the most beautiful beach resorts in the Caribbean. Your first glance from the gangplank is a Caribbean hotel of the luxury class – the Little Dix Bay.

Accommodation & Amenities
The Ocean View rooms stand alone on one of the fantastic white beaches and offer a wonderful view of the crystal-clear sea. The Garden View rooms, from which guests look out over the surrounding tropical gardens, are equally beautiful. Each room has a balcony or terrace and air-conditioning.

Premium- and Deluxe cottages are comfortable, small Caribbean-style houses. The interior furnishings were renewed recently and consist of local handmade wooden-, bamboo- and rattan furniture and textiles that create an exotic atmosphere. The first-class service in Hotel Little Dix Bay and exceptional events such as the popular dinner-evenings ensure a pleasant stay. Creole and international dishes are served in the three restaurants The Pavilion, The Sugar Mill and the Beach Grill.

Activities
Couples are able to go water-skiing together, explore the astounding undersea world while snorkelling and diving, go sailing or use the modern tennis-complex with its seven tennis-courts.

The most modern equipment and the assistance of professional trainers are available in the spacious gym. You can hire a jeep to explore the area on your own. The resort will also be offering recuperation for body and mind in a new spa-centre from the end of 2002. You can then allow yourself to be spoilt there with relaxing traditional Caribbean treatments.

Honeymoon extras/wedding
A bottle of local rum as a welcoming gift. Honeymooners can reserve a suite with a separate bedroom and living-room.

Prices/addresses
An overnight stay costs from £ 89 per person, depending on the category.

Little Dix Bay, P.O. Box 70
Virgin Gorda
British Virgin Islands
Tel: 001-284-495 55 55
Fax: 001-284-495 56 51

U.S. Virgin Islands

Each of the U.S. Virgin Islands is unique in its own way: St. Croix, the largest, is fascinating because of its varied landscape and testimonies to the historical past; busy St. Thomas is a paradise for water-sport fans. St. John, the island with the least number of holiday-travellers and the most dreamlike, is renowned for its impressive nature parks.

Caneel Bay*****

Water-sports paradise on a fantastic island
St. John, U.S. Virgin Islands

The Rosewood Resort features seven pristine white sand beaches on a secluded 170-acre peninsula. Ferry service on Monday, Wednesday and Friday to Little Dix Bay make island-hopping between luxury-class beach resorts possible.

Accommodation & Amenities
The resort's 166 rooms gaze upon the lush tropical gardens and the turqoise-blue Caribbean Sea. The rooms have been completely renovated with handcrafted furniture and richly woven fabrics. Each of them is equipped with air-conditioning and a ceiling-fan so that they always have a pleasant temperature.

The hotel's own restaurants, Turtle Bay Estate House, Equator Restaurant and Caneel Bay Beach Terrace serve an abundance of highly-varied delicacies and afford space for romantic evening dinners. The two bars lure guests to cocktails in a breathtaking atmosphere after sunset.

Activities
Aquatic sports are a major feature of this hotel. You can go sailing or kayaking and discover the underwater world while diving and snorkelling. You may exercise in the fitness centre, take a bath in the inviting swimming-pool or engage in a match on one of the eleven tennis-courts. Naturally, you can also book various wellness treatments such as relaxing, energizing massages. Boats and jeeps for individual, memorable exploratory excursions are for hire.

Honeymoon extras
A bottle of domestic champagne and welcome note.

Prices/addresses
A night costs from £ 98 per person, depending on room-category.

Caneel Bay, P.O. Box 720
Cruz Bay, St. John
U.S.V.I. 00831-0720
Tel: +1-340-776 61 11
Fax: +1-340-693 82 80

Weddings in Paradise

Planning a wedding can be time-consuming, and occasionally nerve-racking. And often the ceremonies in the local registry office last only a few minutes. Marry abroad and your registry office wedding in combination with the honeymoon can be an enjoyable, special experience! That is why more and more couples want to tie the wedding knot far from home. Later, many of them follow it up with a church wedding and a party with their family and friends in their home town.

Some engaged couples desire an exclusive and private atmosphere with a religious ceremony abroad. Other couples, who have already been married, search for that special setting for their next wedding, others for the reaffirmation of vows or an anniversary blessing.

All of these engaged couples have in common the wish for a carefree wedding day and to enjoy the wedding ceremony. To get married with the help of a specialist tour operator not only means to be relieved of the organization of details like the bridal bouquet or wedding limousine, but also from the professional handling of all formalities that are necessary for the legalisation of the foreign marriage.

ANSWERS TO SOME IMPORTANT QUESTIONS

When do you have to book?

Generally as early as possible, to give your tour operator the chance to meet your special wishes. The deadline for the announcement for a wedding varies from destination to destination - between four weeks and few days before. In some countries you can get the wedding licence even on the day. In general, registry office weddings are not available at weekends.

Where does the wedding take place?

All the beach hotels described in this book offer assistance with the organization of the registry office wedding on the beach, and in in the resort. Some hotels have a specially dedicated place in the hotel such as a wedding suite, a gazebo or a pavillon. Depending on the destination, weddings can also be organized in a beautifully decorated registry office, on yachts or in historic colonial buildings. For church weddings, you can have a chapel or church of your denomination, as agreed with your home parish.

Who will celebrate the wedding?

In many countries civil weddings are celebrated by a local registrar as in The Seychelles and Mauritius, or by a Justice of the Peace as in Barbados. In destinations like Hawaii or Fiji, ministers have the official licence to celebrate and legalise weddings. The wedding addresses are delivered within a religious atmosphere, however, the weddings are non-denominational. For church weddings, you can request a local minister of your religious denomination.

Which documents are necessary?

The registry office wedding is regulated by the laws of the destination and these which vary from country to country. In Hawaii engaged couples only need a passport, the authorities in The Seychelles and Mauritius additionally need the birth certificates of the couple and, in case of divorced persons, the certified decree. Specialist tour operators can give detailed information about the relevant countries and organize valid translations of documents, if required.

It is not necessary to give an additional notice of an intended overseas marriage at the registry office in your home town.

Is the wedding legally recognized in the UK?

For marriages solemnised in accordance with the laws of the foreign country, there is no reason to believe that it would not be valid in the UK. Accordingly, you are legally bound by marriage laws from the wedding date shown in the marriage certificate. For the UK, there is no further legalisation necessary following a marriage abroad.

What has to be done after arriving back home?

Though your foreign wedding cannot be registered in the UK, for British citizens who live in the UK and hold valid full British passports under the Foreign Marriage Order of 1970, a record of an overseas marriage, by deposit of the marriage certificate, can be kept at:

The Office of National Statistics (ONS)
General Register Office
Overseas Section, Snedly Hydro
Trafalgar Road
Southport, PR8 2HH
Tel: 0151-471 42 00

This record facility is a means of readily obtaining further copies of the marriage certificate in the UK, rather than from the authorities overseas where the wedding took place. This is not compulsory and does not affect the validity of the marriage. It is not available for marriages which have taken place in Commonwealth countries. If you wish to apply for the deposit of your foreign marriage certificate, please contact:

The Foreign and Commonwealth Office
Consular Division
1 Palace Street
London SW1E 5HE
Tel: 020-72 38 45 67

The mailing of the documents is not subject to a time limit, however the original or a photocopy certified by the issuing authorities must be sent. When an application for copies is made, you will receive certified photocopies, issued under the seal of the General Register Office, and the original certificate will retained at the ONS.

Namechanges, marriage laws and marriage contracts follow the laws of which country?

Generally speaking, these regulations follow the laws of the country where the married couple will have their main residence. For actual and detailed information on specific countries, you should take legal advice from a British lawyer, the ONS or the Foreign and Commonwealth Office.

Where can a "Paradise Wedding" be booked?

Hotel weddings organized by operators can be found in the brochures of tour operators such as Kuoni Travel and Thomson Holidays, and can be booked through most travel agencies. The specialist tour operator with extensive experience for planning and arranging honeymoon travel and organising various wedding arrangements in many overseas countries is Infinity:

Infinity Specialist Tours Ltd.
71a Bell Street
Henley-on-Thames Oxon. RG9 2BD
Tel: 01491-571545
Fax: 01491-636159
e-mail : info@infinitytours.co.uk
www.world-wide-weddings.com

Index

Imprint

Publisher: Infinity Reise Consulting
COMPANIONS GmbH
Rödingsmarkt 9, D-20459 Hamburg,
Tel. 040-306 04-600, Fax 306 04-690
E-Mail: info@companions.de

Author: Ulrich Bieber
Translation: Oscar Schultz-Edwards
Editor-In-Chief: Christina Dickel
Proofreader: Gillian Morris
Designer: Cornelia Prott
Titelphoto: J. P. Fruchet/Getty Images
Printed and bound: Druckerei zu Altenburg

Photos courtesy of:
Silvia Weiss (Portrait p. 1); Carin Behrens (p. 6/7); John Foxx (p. 15, 78); Project Photos (p. 10, 20/21, 26, 29, 34/35, 72, 76/77, 88, 92/93, 94); Kerzner International Resorts (p. 32, 33, 52, 54, 56, 57); PhotoDisc (p. 2 above, 37); Constance Hotels Mauritius (p. 66, 67)
Illustrations: Image Club Graphics
All further photos were kindly provided by the named hotels and airlines.

ISBN 3-89740-385-4

We thank Johnny Kusnadi, Gerald Fitzpatrick, Guy Fotherby and all others involved in producing this book.